HEART SPEAKS TO HEART

Heart Speaks to Heart

THE STORY OF BLESSED
JOHN HENRY NEWMAN

Dermot Mansfield SJ

VERITAS

Published 2010 by
Veritas Publications
7–8 Lower Abbey Street
Dublin 1
Ireland

publications@veritas.ie
www.veritas.ie

ISBN 978-1-84730-242-7

10 9 8 7 6 5 4 3 2

A catalogue record for this book is available from the British Library.

Designed by Lir Mac Cárthaigh
Printed in Ireland by Hudson Killeen Ltd, Dublin

Veritas books are printed on paper made from the wood pulp of managed forests. For every tree felled, at least one tree is planted, thereby renewing natural resources.

— CONTENTS —

*For Mary Sheehy
and to the memory of
Brocard Mansfield* ODC

— INTRODUCTION —

JOHN HENRY NEWMAN, now declared Blessed by the Catholic Church, had one of the most eventful and interesting lives in modern times, spanning the greater part of the nineteenth century. Born in London in 1801, he would spend many years at Oxford and a few at nearby Littlemore. Then apart from a stay in Rome, and some of the 1850s lived in Dublin, he would spend the rest of his long life in Birmingham, dying in that industrial city in 1890. Perhaps at first glance those dates make him seem as belonging to the far distant past – with a whole century intervening between his one and our own – but in important respects Newman can become almost a contemporary figure, speaking directly to us, with a living voice that is still fresh.

For one thing, he was part of a greatly changing environment, as the Industrial Revolution took hold in Britain, with its endless engineering developments, its steam power, leading to an explosion of travel and communication, and out of which the world – certainly the Western world – would evolve into the one we experience now. And Newman himself, like many of his English contemporaries, not only lived through those momentous changes, but also found himself having to change and adapt throughout the whole course of his life.

The earlier and most formative half of his years was spent in the Anglican Church, and the second half was lived in the Catholic Church, all of that containing for him both continuity and upheaval, much searching, and a sifting and weighing of things found. Above all, there was from early on in his life a sense of God; an awareness of the living God before him, calling out to him, and leading him forward, both through dark days and bright ones. That sense of God's presence was uppermost for him, and it was apparent to his many true friends, who valued him both for his down-to-earth humanity, and for his unique ability to inspire and to guide. Furthermore, it was allied to a greatness of mind, which was courageously won, and was in turn brought to bear on many issues and questions of faith.

For these reasons, and for many more, it can be stated that Newman is worth our attention today. He is one of the great luminaries of the modern era. Any study of him will repay our efforts handsomely, and help our living in what is admittedly a very different world – but one which in some respects he could foresee prophetically in outline. It is because of what I believe is his immense value for us that these chapters are offered to the interested reader. Whether you are looking to Newman for the first time, or wish to refresh your understanding or perhaps gain some further insight into him, it is my hope that you will be enriched by the person whose presence is intended to fill these pages.

I am conscious of many people who have helped me in getting this book together. Mary Sheehy, to whom it is dedicated, constantly encouraged me with her great interest. Thomas Morrissey, in my own Jesuit community, who has been a prolific writer, especially on some notable figures in Irish Church history, provided me with helpful advice and some useful material. Paul Andrews, another Jesuit confrere, especially believed that I could write this book. Teresa Iglesias and Anne McNeill, in the Newman Research Library at Newman House on St Stephen's Green, generously gave me access to the huge collection there, as did Mary Glennon and her staff at the Milltown Park Jesuit Library. Another library, incidentally, with useful material included our own one here at Manresa House, Dublin. I have to thank, of course, my own Jesuit confreres in allowing me so much time over the past while to read and research and prepare these chapters. As well, many years ago, the late Gerard Tracey, Archivist at the Birmingham Oratory, was kind and welcoming to me when I was preparing a Licentiate dissertation on Newman's Anglican sermons. And two other figures from the past must be mentioned, Fr Edward Fitzgerald SJ, the best of friends and a keen reader of Newman, and especially Fr Brocard Mansfield ODC, my uncle, who first introduced me to Newman in 1963. To him I am especially grateful. I retain the fondest of memories of my first visit to Newman's Oxford, and to Littlemore, in 1968, in my uncle's company. To Donna Doherty, commissioning editor at Veritas Publications, who asked me to write this book, I am of course indebted. I also wish to thank Caitríona Clarke, Manager of Publications of Veritas, for her help.

DERMOT MANSFIELD
August 2010

— ABBREVIATIONS —

Apo	*Apologia pro Vita Sua*
Ari	*Arians of the Fourth Century*
AW	*Autobiographical Writings*
Dev	*Development of Christian Doctrine*
Diff	*Difficulties felt by Anglicans in Catholic Teaching*
GA	*Grammar of Assent*
Idea	*Idea of a University*
Jfc	*Lectures on the Doctrine of Justification*
LD	*Letters and Diaries of John Henry Newman*
PS	*Parochial and Plain Sermons*
SD	*Sermons on Subjects of the Day*
SVO	*Sermons Preached on Various Occasions*
US	*Fifteen Sermons Preached before the University of Oxford*
VM	*The Via Media of the Anglican Church*

Apart from the *Autobiographical Writings* and the *Letters and Diaries*, the references are to the uniform edition of Newman's works, which he collected between 1869 and 1881. These were published by Longmans, Green and Co. until the stock was destroyed in World War II. Any exceptions, or other references, will be mentioned.

— CHAPTER I —

The Formative Anglican Years

B Y THE STANDARDS of the time – and indeed in certain respects those of our own – Newman's family background and upbringing was quite privileged. Born at 80 Old Broad Street in the City of London on 21 February 1801, John Henry was the eldest of six children, divided equally between boys and girls making up the family of John Newman and Jemima Fourdrinier. His father was the son of a grocer, of humble ancestry in East Anglia, and had managed to do well for himself as a partner in a small banking firm. His mother however, whose background was French, came from a more prosperous family of paper manufacturers, who were of Protestant Huguenot stock and had come to England via Holland to escape persecution. Soon after their first child's birth, they moved west to 17 Southampton Street (now Southampton Place), in Bloomsbury, as gradually the family expanded to include Charles, Harriet, Frank, young Jemima and Mary. They also took Grey Court House, at Ham near Richmond, as their country house for a number of years. It was a wonderful place for young John Henry, his 'Paradise', where he remembered long after hearing from his crib the soft sound of the scythe cutting the grass outside, the house and setting often being in his dreams.

The Newmans were evidently a happy couple, delighting in their lively and adventurous growing children. As for religion, they were members of the Anglican Established Church, John holding moderate and open-minded views, and suspicious of anything enthusiastic. Jemima however was devoutly religious, and wished in particular to inculcate an attachment to and love of the Bible in her family. With regard to education, they were keen to get the best possible for John Henry, who at the age of seven was sent as a boarder to the flourishing Great Ealing School, run by Dr George Nicholas, a kind and warm family friend. It was an excellent choice, as the school continued the sense of security the boy had found at home, while also providing him with an enlightened and stimulating education, rounded out by the performance of plays, debating and music, as well as boating, bathing and riding. A quick learner, he was also a leader among some of the boys, starting a club and founding school newspapers, while in his spare time devouring the Waverley novels of Sir Walter Scott as they came out. When he was ten, his father bought him a violin, and with the help of his music teacher he was soon accomplished in its use – playing, among other works, sonatas by the contemporary Beethoven, a love for whom stayed with him.

There were however tumultuous distant events in Europe that would impinge upon the relatively enclosed world he knew then. As a small child in bed at Ham in October 1805, John Henry had watched the candles lighting at the windows to honour the naval victory at Trafalgar, which removed the threat of invasion by Napoleon. But early in 1816 his secure school and family existence was shattered when, in the aftermath of the ending of the Napoleonic wars, his father's bank was among a number that failed. It was a crushing blow. Although managing to pay back all his depositors, the elder Newman's confidence never recovered, and the family fortunes went steadily downhill. That summer, it was decided that their fifteen-year-old son should remain over the holidays in the school at Ealing because of the upheaval at home, which he did. Lonely and desolate, he fell seriously ill for a time. But then a great change came over him, leading to a deep appreciation of Christian faith, and of a kind that would remain in essence with him over his whole lifetime.

Although brought up as an Anglican, and conventionally observant in his religion, the young Newman in truth was at a critical stage in his development. As would have been the case with some other young enquiring people then, he had been toying to some extent with the sceptical literature of the time, wondering about the immortality of the soul, and thinking that perhaps it would be best 'to be virtuous but not religious'. But now this unexpected blow to his family, and his own illness, led him into completely new and uncharted territory, where he believed that God 'mercifully touched his heart', changing him in a radical way.

Newman always looked back with gratitude to the young clergyman, Walter Mayers, who taught at the school, and who was on hand that summer and into the autumn and winter of 1816 to guide him. Many years later, in 1864, when as a Catholic he wrote the classic account of his religious development in the *Apologia pro Vita Sua*, he spoke of this experience as an 'inward conversion', one that took place over the final five months of 1816. In particular, and reiterating a previous childhood mistrust of material phenomena around him, he was brought to rest 'in the thought of two and only two absolutely and luminously self-evident beings, myself and my Creator.'[1]

He was greatly helped by the books Mayers lent him, especially *The Force of Truth* (1779) by Thomas Scott. What made a great impression on him was Scott's teaching on the Blessed Trinity, allied to what he learned then about the Incarnation and the Redemption. These great central truths of the Christian faith became vividly real for him. Personally, he saw himself now as a sinful but redeemed creature before God, and in consequence drawn in thankfulness to serve God with all he had. In this way there came about what has been described as his earnest quest for holiness, and especially through the influence of Thomas Scott. And in the *Apologia* he said that 'for years I used almost as proverbs what I considered to be the scope and issue of his doctrine, "holiness rather than peace", and "growth the only evidence of life"'.[2]

It is worthy of note that both Newman's mentor Walter Mayers and the author Thomas Scott were exemplars of the Evangelical Revival in the Church of England. Both of these had undergone the kind of conversion experience considered central to Evangelicalism – and in a way that was what Newman underwent during those months. The Evangelical Revival had begun in the previous century in England as an enthusiastic religious movement, embracing rich and poor, and partly in reaction to what was felt to be the uninspiring mainstream life of the Established Church. A great emphasis was placed on scripture, and on preaching as the means by which the Holy Spirit largely operated in bringing about the salvation of souls. But it was the personal experience of conversion that was considered the mark of salvation, as celebrated for instance in the hymn 'Amazing Grace' by John Newton, another well-known Evangelical cleric of the time. Powerful in its effects on a great many people, Evangelicalism was responsible for a renewed vitality within the Church of England, while also, through John Wesley and others, leading to the separate and more populist movement of Methodism.

Newman, then, as a thoughtful young fifteen-year-old, was profoundly influenced by this Revival. There were however aspects to his Evangelical outlook that would soon change. Thus he held for a time the belief that the Pope was anti-Christ, as was thought in some Protestant circles to have been predicted in the Books of Daniel and Revelation. And for a short while he considered as true the Calvinist tenet of double predestination: that through God's mercy some are chosen to eternal life, while others are left unredeemed and therefore 'predestined' to eternal loss. More positively, there was the wide theological horizon opened up, centred on the doctrine of the Trinity and the Incarnation, and which he would keep before him through devotion to the Athanasian Creed. It was filled out by long readings from the Fathers, St Augustine and others, which he found in the Evangelical *History of the Church of Christ* by Joseph Milner. Also, what he called in the *Apologia* the 'main Catholic doctrine of the warfare between the city of God and the powers of darkness' was impressed upon him from another source. That dramatic and apocalyptic scenario was one that would always be there for him, and a motivation for the concerns engaging him throughout his life.

At the heart of it all was the sense of being personally chosen by God – and so he set out with all he had to live day by day in God's presence. Moreover, 'a deep imagination', as he called it, took hold of him that autumn: that it was God's will he should live a single life. This was a rare enough ideal in Protestantism, and was much misunderstood when he mentioned it later in the *Apologia*. But such was the awareness he had of God's presence and calling, setting him apart, that the notion for him was very real. It was one which would, except for a few times of doubt and testing, remain with him onwards in his Anglican life, and through the Catholic phase beyond.

Life moved on for him quickly. His father, despite his precarious financial situation, was determined to send his eldest son to university. In June 1817, aged just sixteen, John Henry travelled to historic Oxford, with its beautiful surrounds, cradled by the River Isis (as the Thames is known there) and its tributary, the Cherwell. He took up residence in Trinity College, to which he had gained admittance the previous December. A large world began to open out for him from then onward through his studies, which alongside the classics and mathematics were quite wide-ranging, and through meeting new companions. Newman was always someone who made friends, and some of those he made in the early years at Oxford would remain so for life – especially John Bowden, whom he met the very first day he came into residence. Although Bowden was three years older, the two of them became inseparable companions during their years in Trinity.

The following year he won a college scholarship for nine years, which relieved the financial pressure on his father. Although able to enjoy life, he stood back firmly from the drinking culture the gentlemen students tried at times to force upon him, which gained him the respect of some. In 1820 he took his degree examinations, but lost his nerve during them and did badly as a result. At nineteen, he was three years younger than most who took a degree, and had overworked, without adequate supervision. His family were a big support to him afterwards – especially his father, even though he was now heading towards bankruptcy, with the house in Southampton Street and its contents having to be sold, and the family then moving into successively cheaper lodgings in London.

But still John Henry had a degree, and his scholarship, and so could continue. With confidence in his ability, which others shared, he hoped he could eventually become a Fellow of Oriel College, which was pre-eminent in Oxford at that time. He let his enquiring mind roam freely, with serious incursions into music composition and astronomy; also into the natural sciences, philosophy, history, Hebrew and Arabic, and law. Then at Easter 1822 he took the examinations for Oriel, thinking this would be only a trial attempt. But he found himself doing well as the days went on, and felt helped by the words in the stained-glass window in the hall, *'Pie repone te'*, 'lovingly rest yourself'. On 12 April he learned he had been successful, and joining the names of Fellows which were then among the most prestigious in the university, he was now an equal among the academics making up the community of Oriel, with a place for life if need be, and an income. The day of his election he later called 'of all days the most memorable. It raised me from obscurity and need to competency and reputation.'[3] It also meant he could support his impoverished family, in their very straitened circumstances, and with his father now irreversibly declining in health.

Intellectually, the time ahead in Oriel was profoundly significant. Its leading lights were around him, including the Provost Edward Copleston, John Keble, Richard Whately, Edward Hawkins and John Davison. From the first, he found himself being challenged and drawn out by them, especially by Richard Whately, who was later to be Archbishop of Dublin, and Edward Hawkins, Vicar of the University Church of St Mary the Virgin. In their company, Newman learned to enter into the views of others, while also to think resolutely for himself and weigh up opinions in a clear-headed way. It was an exciting and liberating atmosphere, not without its temptations, as he put it later, 'to prefer intellectual excellence to moral'. Yet he had gradually set his sights on seeking Anglican orders, and on 13 June 1824 he was ordained deacon. 'I am thine, O Lord', he wrote in his journal that day, as he pondered the idea of 'giving up all for God'. And the following day he added, 'I have the responsibility of souls on me to the day of my death.'[4] And indeed, the rest of his life could be read in the light of that responsibility.

He took on the curacy of the parish of St Clement across the bridge over the Cherwell at Magdalen College. There, many of the people were poor, and he soon started on rounds of visiting them, especially the sick, and began regular preaching. He also was instrumental in raising substantial money to build a new church, to replace the old one in which he officiated. His first sermon, actually in a distant country church where his former guide Walter Mayers was curate, was on the text: 'Man goeth forth to his work and to his labour until the evening' (Ps 104). Many years later it was to be the text of his last Anglican sermon.

That September his father died, and he now became the breadwinner for his whole family. He wrote at the time: 'When I die shall I be followed to the grave by my children? My mother said the other day she hoped to live to see me married, but I think I shall either die within a College walls, or a Missionary in a foreign land – no matter where, so that I die in Christ.'[5]

As he visited his parishioners in their homes, the young pastor came up against hard facts, which ran counter to the simplistic Evangelical way of classifying humanity as either subject to darkness or light. He found himself meeting many different kinds of people, and, inconsistent though he found them to be on aspects of faith, he could not help but admit that grace was at work in their lives. Edward Hawkins too criticised his initial preaching on conversion as naïve, in the way he divided people into categories of nominal and real Christianity, and on how he insisted on the process of conversion, with a clear-cut division between those who either had or had not undergone the experience. Soon the narrow mentality of Evangelicalism gave way, as his own good sense and his concern for truth led him to see that it was to an extent an unreal system. 'What shall I do?' he exclaimed in his journal after conversation with an argumentative Calvinist couple, 'I *really* desire the truth.'[6]

On 25 May 1825 he was ordained priest. In addition he was by now Vice-Principal of St Alban's Hall, a residence for students, and was occupied as a College Tutor, raising additional money to support his family and get his brother Frank through university. All these demands were such that at Easter 1826 he gave up St Clement's, feeling his talents at that point lay in tutoring and in what were to him the pastoral responsibilities for the young university men under his charge. With them, especially the gentlemen commoners, he had a reputation for kindness, but steely determination in tackling low standards, especially any dissipation on the few occasions when they were expected to take Holy Communion.

One unusual companion of his for a time at Oriel was the Spaniard Blanco White, of Irish descent, who had been a Roman Catholic priest, Canon of Seville Cathedral, before taking on the Liberal cause and then entering the Anglican ministry. With Newman he shared a love of the violin, and together they were involved in playing Beethoven's Quartets. But whatever liberal ideas they had in common did not last. And soon BlancoWhite was to lose his belief in the divinity of Christ, and head via Unitariansim into Pantheism. For Newman, the story of his loss of belief would provide much food for thought.

His own move in a very different direction would be helped by a series of events. In the autumn of 1827 he became quite ill for a time, and suffered a serious loss of confidence, mainly due to overwork. Worse was to come. Over the Christmas and New Year holidays he went home to be with his family, which he had arranged to get settled at Brighton. Suddenly, on the eve of Epiphany, his youngest sister Mary took ill and died. Only nineteen, she had been very close to her eldest brother. Maria Giberne, a friend of the family (and who would have a lifelong loyalty to John Henry), was there at the time, and saw the effect it had on him. He was utterly shocked by what had happened, and often afterwards, even into old age, tears came to his eyes when he thought of Mary. He struggled to believe that it was all within God's providence, and the blow revived in him his deep sense of the unseen world surrounding our own, and more real than the material one we touch. As he wrote to his sister Jemima months later, after riding out from Oxford in the countryside: 'Dear Mary seems embodied in every tree and hid behind every hill. What a veil and curtain this world of sense is! Beautiful, but still a veil.'[7] And both his own illness and Mary's loss shocked him out of a reliance on intellectual prowess and into a deeper dependence in faith on God's designs.

Much more happened in those early months of 1828. Edward Copleston had departed from Oriel, on becoming Bishop of Llandaff. Hawkins was now elected Provost, and Newman went on to succeed him as vicar of the lovely church of St Mary's, his institution taking place on 14 March. Centrally situated, with a seventeenth-century statue of the Virgin and Child over its entrance on the High Street, its impressive spire then as now dominated Oxford. But despite its title as the University Church, the normal congregation at St Mary's was made up largely of the families of shopkeepers, tradesmen and servants in the colleges, and soon Newman was busy teaching catechism to their children. In time however, and since he was also on occasion official preacher to the university, his sermons there would attract a wider and more learned audience – and when published, would have a profound effect upon many of a whole generation in England and further afield.

Throughout, there was a whole pattern of enquiry and growth going on in Newman's religious understanding. Already, at the time of his Evangelical conversion, his Trinitarian faith began to provide him with a vision of the great components of revealed truth, centred on the meaning of the Incarnation and our Redemption. Then Hawkins helped to wean him off his emphasis on the experience of conversion itself, and to recognise the efficacy of Baptism. Hawkins too supplemented his reverence for Scripture by pointing to the role of Church tradition in its interpretation. And by his own reading, especially of Bishop Butler's *Analogy of Religion*, he began to acquire a strong sense of the Church as 'the oracle of truth and pattern of sanctity', so that even in his early preaching at St Clement's he was insisting on the visible nature of the Church, and its being 'Catholic' and 'Apostolic'.

And now, other figures at Oriel College began to exercise a decisive influence on him – but from a different standpoint, that of the traditional High Church strand of Anglicanism. Thus he had already come to admire Edward Bouverie Pusey, elected to Oriel in 1823, who went on to pursue further studies in Germany and would become Professor of Hebrew at Oxford. In 1827 Pusey, at his request, brought him back folio editions of the Greek and Latin Fathers from

Germany, and starting in the summer of 1828 he began reading them systematically. Already enamoured by his initial reading of excerpts of Augustine and Ambrose and others in 1816, Newman now entered into a long process of assimilating the patristic writings, believing that the early centuries offered the great normative interpretation of Christian revelation and life. He also came close to two other significant people, Hurrell Froude, elected a Fellow in 1826, and John Keble, whom he had known a little but revered greatly since beginning at Oriel. The older and self-effacing Keble, who had never attended school before coming to Oxford, had been the most brilliant student of his generation. He had joined Oriel in 1811, was now Professor of Poetry, and was author of the much-loved collection of hymns and religious poetry, *The Christian Year*, verses from which Newman's sister Mary had been repeating by heart as she lay dying.

People like these, and other High Churchmen, whom the formerly Evangelical Newman came to know, paved the way for him to understand their classical predecessors, namely the major Anglican theologians, or 'divines', as they were known, from the late sixteenth and seventeenth centuries. Many of those earlier figures, especially from the Caroline era – the reigns of Charles I and Charles II – had also been patristic scholars, although it would be some time yet before Newman made an intimate acquaintance with their writings. Keble and Pusey in particular, with their learning, represented these for Newman. Hurrell Froude in turn was the disciple of Keble. He said later that 'the one good thing' he did in life was to bring Keble and Newman to understand each other.

Froude did more than that, however. He helped Newman to look beyond even the Reformation itself, and acquire some sympathy with the Church of Rome, especially in its medieval period. This was significant, and would lead to the evaporation of his idea of the Pope as Anti-Christ. He brought him as well to accept the doctrine of the Real Presence and to have devotion to the Blessed Virgin. He also held before him in a new light the ideal of priestly celibacy. This was at a time when Newman witnessed some deeply happy marriages, especially John Bowden's, which was to Elizabeth Swinburne, from a well-known formerly Catholic family in Northumberland. Pusey also at this time married Maria Barker, who in turn became friendly with Newman. At one point, Newman found himself attracted by Froude's lovely sisters, when staying at their father's home in Devon. But while he accepted that marriage and family life suited priests in settled country parsonages, he believed that those like himself who were involved in more missionary situations, whether at home or abroad, should remain single.

In fact, this was how Newman saw himself engaged at this time. He was fast becoming the centre of an active and talented group, and therefore in a situation which required of him a high degree of personal commitment. Among these companions was the future High Church theologian, Robert Wilberforce, who with Froude had become a Fellow of Oriel in 1826. Others came from among Newman's most talented pupils, such as Frederic Rogers, and Henry Wilberforce, the younger brother of Robert – sons of the great William Wilberforce, the Evangelical slave emancipator. All of them were being brought together in espousing the cause of the Church, which they felt was coming under threat from a variety of sources. There was certainly a widespread alienation from Anglicanism at this time, occurring in the growing industrial cities and towns. And, in the aftermath of the granting of Catholic Emancipation in 1829, a new reforming Whig government had replaced the Tories, who were determined to trim the Established Church's outmoded privileges and influence. But while ecclesiastical power and prestige were likewise anathema to High Church people like Keble and Newman, in principle they were opposed to government interference. They were also united against what they saw as a growing Liberal spirit in Oxford and elsewhere in England, fuelled by political and philosophical developments in Europe – and which was the enemy of the orthodoxy they were now espousing. For them, the Liberal approach posed a real threat to revealed religion, exalting the independent rational mind as the proud arbiter of truth, and leading to a decay of trust in religious authority.

Hawkins and Whately naturally were alarmed at what was to them the growing reactionary attitude of their young former protégé. Whately believed Newman had deserted the Liberal cause and was assuming an orthodox mantle because he was ambitious for advancement in the Church. And Hawkins, as Provost, considering in any case that Newman's pastoral approach to academic tutoring was out of place, took action by stopping his supply of pupils, so that in 1830 his role as College Tutor was ended, depriving him of much-needed income for his family. He still had the main responsibility for his mother and sisters, who at this time moved close to him, setting up house in the riverside village of Iffley, which was near Littlemore, an outlying district of his parish.

In the spring of 1831 he began work on a study of the Council of Nicea, having been invited to contribute to the proposed publication of a theological library on the early Councils of the Church. 'It was to launch myself on an ocean with currents innumerable,' he wrote in the *Apologia*.[8] The outcome was his first book, completed in 1832, and published the following year, not as part of the proposed series, but as a volume on its own entitled *The Arians of the Fourth Century*. It dealt with the controversies of the crucial period surrounding the Council of Nicea (325), and especially with the divisions coming in its wake. Among other things, it included what is still a fine outline of the scriptural and theological doctrine of the Trinity.[9] Above all, the Church of Alexandria became the focus of Newman's study, which was then, as he saw it, 'the natural mediator between East and West', and personified in the towering figure of its bishop St Athanasius, 'who, after the Apostles, has been a principal instrument, by which the sacred truths of Christianity have been conveyed and secured to the world.'[10]

His book was a major historical and theological treatise, therefore, and intended to show in an exemplary light the perennial Catholic dimension of the Church. This was a reality growing powerfully in his mind and heart. He was beginning to see very clearly that 'there was something greater than the Established Church, and that was the Church Catholic and Apostolic, set up from the beginning, of which she was both the local presence and the organ. She was nothing, unless she was this.'[11] Throughout, his sermons were attracting more and more notice. Two important ones, but preached at Tunbridge Wells, were entitled 'Knowledge of God's will without Obedience' and 'The Religion of the Day', where he showed that the 'religion' of civilisation was becoming a substitute for authentic Christianity. One interesting group of sermons at St Mary's presented fascinating moral portraits of key Old Testament personalities: Abraham, Moses, Saul, David, Solomon and Jeroboam. He also delivered during 1830–1832 eight official University Sermons, where he set out the principles he was developing for a philosophy of religion. Especially in 'The Influence of Natural and Revealed Religion' he treated the subject of conscience – a theme that would occupy him onwards through his life. Conscience for him, as he said then, was really the religious sense within us, pointing to 'a Supreme Power, claiming our habitual obedience', and also the moral sense, providing us with 'the inward law of right and wrong'. It is at the source of Natural Religion, therefore, but needing to be complemented by the great personal object of our devotion and worship given in Revealed Religion.[12]

Meanwhile his personal quest continued, as subsequent events led to a spiritual crisis, on which he would often ponder. Froude was diagnosed with tuberculosis, and his father, Archdeacon Froude, who had already lost his wife and another son to the disease, was anxious to take Hurrell to the warmer climate of the Mediterranean in the winter of 1832–1833. The Froudes asked Newman to accompany them, and needing a break after the effort of writing his book on the Arians, he agreed to do so. Setting out from Falmouth on their long sea voyage, they made their way to Corfu, visiting also Malta, Palermo, Naples and finally Rome. Despite his theological Catholic sympathies, much of what Newman saw of contemporary Roman Catholicism did not appeal to him. In Rome itself, they received news that the government at home was moving to abolish some of the Irish Anglican bishoprics, and were incensed, intending to act resolutely when they returned to England. Before leaving, they made personal contact with the Roman church by meeting Dr Nicholas Wiseman, Rector of the English College, a man who was to play an important role in Newman's life later on. As they parted, Wiseman expressed the hope that they might visit Rome again – to which Newman was moved to reply, 'We have a work to do in England'.

Clearly, there was a serious challenge awaiting them back in England. As the Froudes started on their journey home, however,

Newman decided to leave them, against their advice. The beauty of Sicily had fascinated him when they were there earlier, and now he was determined to make his way back alone, to view once more its relics of antiquity. But while there, and in the middle of all that enthralled him, he became seriously ill with fever and nearly died. Everything became personally dark for him too, as he found himself entering into a state of personal turmoil and self-recrimination.

He recalled that just before leaving Oxford, he had preached the sermon, 'Wilfulness the Sin of Saul', linking that Old Testament figure to the indifference and disdain being shown in some quarters to the Church. Now in Sicily, as soon as he felt the illness coming on, he began to dread that it was he himself who had committed that sin of wilfulness, despite having professed to be a spiritual leader of others. He felt that much of what he had been trying to do at home was governed by proud self-will. 'I seemed to see more and more my utter hollowness.' He chastised himself in the quarrel with Hawkins over the tutorship: 'Then I bitterly blamed myself, as disrespectful and insulting to the Provost, my superior.' He thought too that he had received the Sacrament at that time in malice and resentment.

Yet, when his fever was at its worst, over ten or eleven days, he also had the thought that God had not abandoned him. He kept on saying to himself, 'I have not sinned against light', and at one moment, 'I had a most consoling overpowering thought of God's electing love, and seemed to feel I was his.' Recovering a little strength, he set out with the help of the local servant he had hired to get to a ship at Palermo, feeling as he travelled that he must shed reliance on self, and go instead on God's way, 'that I must put myself in his path, his way'. Again he fell ill with fever, and was laid up for some weeks – during which he found himself saying over and over to Gennaro, his uncomprehending servant, the words he had said to Wiseman in Rome: 'I have a work to do in England.'[13]

Finally he set sail from Palermo on the first leg of the journey home. Before his illness, throughout the earlier travels he had been writing quite an amount of poetry. And now as he was finally headed home, when the ship was becalmed in the straits of Bonifacio between Corsica and Sardinia, on 16 June 1833 he wrote 'The Pillar of the

Cloud'. It would later, as a hymn, be best known across the Christian denominations by its opening lines:

> Lead, Kindly Light, amid the encircling gloom,
>   Lead Thou me on!
> The night is dark, and I am far from home –
>   Lead Thou me on!
>   Keep Thou my feet; I do not ask to see
> The distant scene, – one step enough for me.
>
>   I was not ever thus, nor pray'd that Thou
>   Shouldst lead me on.
>   I loved to choose and see my path; but now
>   Lead Thou me on!
>   I loved the garish day, and, spite of fears,
> Pride ruled my will: remember not past years.
>
> So long Thy power hath blest me, sure it still
>   Will lead me on,
> O'er moor and fen, o'er crag and torrent, till
>   The night is gone;
> And with the morn those angel faces smile
> Which I have loved long since, and lost awhile.

NOTES

1. *Apo,* p. 4.
2. Ibid., p. 5.
3. *AW,* p. 63.
4. Ibid., pp. 200–1.
5. Ibid., p. 203.
6. Ibid., p. 202; italics here, as elsewhere, in original.
7. *LD,* II, p. 61.
8. *Apo,* p. 26.
9. *Ari,* pp. 151–78.
10. Ibid., pp. 374–5.
11. *Apo,* pp. 31–2.
12. cf. *OUS,* pp. 18–25.
13. cf. *AW,* pp. 121–38.

— CHAPTER 2 —

Leader of the Oxford Movement

LREADY, WHILE NEWMAN was away, a number of able people across the country had been in contact with each other, and were becoming united in their determination to oppose the various moves they felt were threatening the future of the Church. On 9 July 1833 a rejuvenated Newman arrived back from his travels at his mother's house. On the following Sunday, 14 July, John Keble preached in St Mary's a sermon on 'National Apostasy', portraying an England in danger of abandoning its ancient allegiance to Christ and Church. This day and event Newman ever afterwards kept as the start of what became known as the Oxford Movement.

Soon meetings were held, and an association began to form. Newman himself was not as fully involved with these as some others were – 'living movements do not come out of committees, nor are great ideas worked out through the post, even though it had been the penny post.'[1] His own initial main contribution was in suggesting that Tracts or pamphlets be written and distributed. He himself wrote the first four in quick succession, calling them *Tracts for the Times*, addressed to clergy and exhorting them to defend the Church, 'for the times are very evil, yet no one speaks against them'. He asked his confreres therefore to uphold their bishops: 'Is it fair, is it dutiful, to suffer our Bishops to stand the brunt of the battle without doing our part to support them?' he asked. They needed help to live up to their high calling – although his evocation of what that could imply may not have received their general episcopal approval: 'And, black event as it would be for the country, yet (as far as they are concerned) we could not wish them a more blessed termination of their course, than the spoiling of their goods, and martyrdom.'

That autumn more and more Tracts appeared, the daring language of the early ones creating much interest. Newman rode about the countryside, giving them into parsonages, while generally they were posted off in bundles to sympathetic clergy further afield, and then distributed by them and others who rallied to the cause. Soon he was writing: 'We are in action from the Isle of Wight to Durham and from Cornwall to Kent.' From being just a few pages at first, the *Tracts for the Times* grew into small treatises, written by various hands but all edited by their founder. They were lent greater authority when Pusey, now Canon of Christchurch and Professor of Hebrew, wrote one. 'He at once gave us a position and a name. Without him we should have had little chance, especially at the early date of 1834, of making any serious resistance to the Liberal aggression.'[2]

All the while, despite a widespread growing personal influence, Newman was also devoting time to his local parish. From the beginning of his time at St Mary's, he had been concerned about the many parishioners in the country area of Littlemore, nearly three miles out on the London road. He walked out regularly to visit them, arranged classes for the teaching of the children, and started to collect money for the building of a church. And when his mother and sisters Jemima and Harriet moved to the village of Iffley nearby, they not only provided a home where he could stay from time to time, but became involved in his work, especially through helping the poorer parishioners. In Oxford itself, and along that road, and around Littlemore, he had become a very familiar figure: he was slightly above average height, bespectacled, having soft, light brown hair, a ruddy face with grey-blue eyes, and prominent nose and full mouth, which seem to have come from his mother's side of the family.

That was the same figure appearing in St Mary's Sunday after Sunday, and whose words spoken there would be in many respects the source of his great authority over the significant years ahead.

Starting from his appointment as vicar in 1828, Newman put much effort into composing the sermons he was expected to give – and the initial sprinkling of ordinary parochial families who came to hear him was gradually supplemented by a large and intent congregation drawn from all parts of the university. On the mornings of Sundays and Saints' days however, he did not usually give the official sermons to the university. Instead, his place was to preach 'plain' sermons on the Sunday afternoons, at the four o'clock service. His influence in preaching was such that many of the college authorities became alarmed, leading them to change times of residence to prevent undergraduates from attending, but without much success.

Many of those listeners would retain lifelong memories of Newman in the pulpit of St Mary's and bear testimony to the lasting effect of his words. He had none of the imposing presence and eloquence expected of noted preachers in those days. He read his text, as was the custom, in a clear but not very strong voice and rather quickly, although pausing from time to time and with occasional emphases according to the meaning. However, he drew out what he had to say from a remarkable knowledge of scripture, together with what people felt was great insight into human conscience and motivation. One of those who heard him was Richard Church – later to be Dean of St Paul's in London and subsequent lifelong friend of Newman. In his classic book *The Oxford Movement* (1891) he wrote of how Newman's words 'made men think of the things which the preacher spoke of, and not of the sermon or the preacher'.[3] Church believed that the Oxford Movement, under the influence of these sermons, brought about a great change in the approach of people's hearts to Christ whose name 'stood no longer for an abstract symbol of doctrine, but for a living Master, who could teach as well as save'.[4]

In March 1834 the first volume of Newman's *Parochial Sermons* appeared in print, and his influence as a result began to spread across the English-speaking world. In some of the sermons chosen for the volume, a stark and typical theme can be seen where Newman remarks on those in comfortable and educated circumstances – who are inclined to keep an eye on what the world thinks of them, and whose religion in consequence is 'a mere civilisation', based on self and the world. The theme can be seen in 'Profession without Practice', 'Promising without Doing' and 'The Self-Wise Enquirer'.

Included also were sermons entitled, 'Knowledge of God's Will without Obedience' and 'The Religion of the Day'. In the latter, Newman speaks of the contemporary enlightened age, and asks, '… what is the world's religion now? It has taken the brighter side of the Gospel – its tidings of comfort, its precepts of love; all darker, deeper views of man's conditions and prospects being comparatively forgotten. This is the religion *natural* to a civilised age, and well has Satan dressed and completed it into an idol of the Truth.' It is a religion where people have 'more or less identified their vision of Christ's kingdom with the elegance and refinement of mere human civilisation' and putting aside the warnings in the Gospel about the narrow gate, 'are ready to embrace the pleasant consoling religion natural to a polished age'. As a great contrast with this, Newman stresses the scriptural words, 'the fear of God is the beginning of wisdom', and 'our God is a consuming fire', and bids us instead to 'approach him with reverence and godly fear … Fear and love must go together; always fear, always love, to your dying day.'[5]

Two more volumes were published in 1835 and 1836 respectively, setting out the great round of recovered Catholic Christian truth, some aspects of which had been long forgotten at that time. The selection in Volume II followed the course of the Church's year, and included important sermons such as 'Faith without Sight', 'The Reverence due to the Blessed Virgin Mary', 'Christ, a Quickening Spirit', 'The Indwelling Spirit', and 'The Gospel, a Trust committed to Us'. Volume III contained a general selection, and included 'A Particular Providence as revealed in the Gospel', 'The Humiliation of the Eternal Son', 'The Church Visible and Invisible', and 'The Gift of the Spirit'.

Naturally the selection in those volumes was small compared to the number of sermons Newman was preaching in St Mary's over those years, where people gathered every Sunday afternoon to listen to him intently as he read the scripture lessons, and then outline their meaning in a way which clearly came from the experience of a life lived in truth and prayer. But it is worth remarking that Newman himself at that time was reserved about the role of preaching. In some private correspondence, for instance, he expressed the view that a preacher ought to be like John the Baptist, whose mission is to prepare his hearers for the mystery of Christ. 'Preaching is not the means of conversion,' he wrote. 'The Church with the Sacraments etc. and the life of good men seem to me the great persuasives of the Gospel.'[6]

There were other fronts on which he was active. Just at the time in 1834 when his first volume of sermons appeared, he had stood for the Professorship of Moral Philosophy. But he was outmanoeuvred politically by Hawkins, who put forward successfully at the last moment the Liberal theologian Renn Dickson Hampden. He was someone with whom Newman would do battle over the next few years, as the Liberals worked to gain the upper hand over the Tractarians and change the character of Oxford as an Anglican foundation. In 1835 Hampden became active in trying to abolish subscription to the Thirty-Nine Articles, the traditional tenets of Anglicanism, required of entrants to the university. He did so on the basis that theological differences were of little consequence among Christians – but his arguments, Newman believed, would tend to 'make a shipwreck of the Christian Faith'. Then in 1836 he was appointed as Regius Professor of Divinity, and although opposed by Newman and Pusey and many others, the prime minister, Lord Melbourne, ensured that the appointment stood. One of Hampden's supporters was a former Oriel man: Thomas Arnold of Rugby School, destined to become its famous headmaster. His strong Liberal and reforming views made him vehemently hostile towards Newman and his friends, whose opposition to Hampden he considered as nothing more than narrow-minded persecution – a view shared by the popular press.

Personally, 1836 was a watershed year for Newman. Keble married quietly, to Charlotte Clarke, his friend since childhood, and moved away to become vicar of the country parish of Hursley, near Winchester. On 28 February Hurrell Froude finally died from consumption, at the age of thirty-three. He had been out of Oxford for a long time, as his illness progressed. Newman had stayed with him some months previously, and now the news of his death affected him deeply. Invited by the Archdeacon to keep some memento from his library, he took away Hurrell's four volumes of the Roman Breviary, which he later began reciting regularly, although leaving out such parts as the invocations to the Virgin Mary which were not allowed by the Anglican Church. He loved its 'majestic and austere' Latin language, and its reliance on the psalms. In the summer he brought out *Tract 75* on the Roman Breviary, 'as embodying the substance of the devotional services of the Church Catholic'.

He also, in effect, lost his own family that year, as well as the place they had provided for him as a home away from Oriel. In April his sister Jemima married John Mozley – a brother of Newman's friend Tom Mozley, who had been his student, and was ordained – and she moved away to Derby with her husband, who took over the family printing business. A few weeks later Mrs Newman collapsed, and after a short illness she died, Harriet and John being with her. Then Harriet went up to Derby to be with the Mozley family, and soon after she was proposed to by Tom, and married him. So it was that Newman suddenly found himself left alone. He had never been that close to his brother Charles, who had separated himself from the family circle early on, embracing atheism and the concerns of the social reformer Robert Owen (he 'beats St Paul hollow', he wrote to John). Although he managed to write some pamphlets on socialism, Charles would fail to make anything of his life, and would depend on his brothers for financial support. And Frank, who earlier had been part of a disastrous Evangelical mission to Persia, was now tending towards Unitarianism, and would end up without any recognisable form of Christian faith. He married around the same time as his sisters and would embark upon a university career in Manchester and London, becoming noted as a speaker on all sorts of contemporary subjects of interest.

After his mother's death, Newman blamed himself for some unresolved misunderstandings – he had felt the same after his father's death. To an extent he was unfair to himself, as both his parents in their different ways had been uncomprehending and anxious about the course his life was taking. But what was special to him was the fact that his mother had laid the foundation stone of his church at Littlemore in the summer of 1835. And he had great happiness when the little Church of Ss Mary and Nicholas was dedicated by the Bishop on 22 September 1836, with his friends gathered, as well as his curate Isaac Williams. There were bunches of flowers all about it, two baptisms were performed, and Newman gave out buns to all the children present. Every year from then onwards the anniversary of Littlemore Church's dedication would be kept as a sacred memory by him, and indeed by his next curate, John Rouse Bloxam – who, although a lifelong Anglican, would always remain devoted to him. A tablet was also put up in the church to the memory of his mother.

Although he was alone, his only home now being his two rooms next to the chapel in Oriel College, Newman's place as leader of the Oxford or Tractarian Movement was becoming more and more evident. He was not however, and would never be, an organiser or great administrator. His way was to be that of a friend and an encouraging presence among like-minded people, who between them in freedom would uphold what was true and act for the best. Inevitably, there would be those who wanted more authoritative planned action, and divisions and estrangements would occur in consequence – both now and later in his Catholic life. Always his approach would be that of personal influence, together with the best articulation possible of the great truths of Catholic Christianity, and the upholding of what it meant to live one's life based on the Gospel and centred on the person of Christ. And if some became impatient with him, there were many more who turned to what he stood for, attracted by what was seen as his human sympathy, humour and simplicity of manner.

In November 1836 the verses he had composed, mainly on his continental journey, were published in a collection entitled *Lyra Apostolica*. They had appeared piecemeal since 1833 in a magazine run by the High Churchman Hugh Rose, who had helped at the beginning of the Movement. Other poems in the collection were by Keble. Isaac Williams, who would become a well-known Tractarian poet, also contributed a number. Although he had no great confidence in his own poetic ability, Newman rightly felt that the

Lyra Apostolica was a worthwhile venture, in portraying the ideals of Tractarianism to a readership then eager for the religious poetry they were offering, and who of course already had been very taken by Keble's best-selling *Christian Year*.

Apart from preaching, Newman had begun on his own initiative to offer lectures, and at the time when he had been denied a professorship. At St Mary's he set up the unused chapel of Adam de Brome (Oriel's medieval founder) as a place in which he could give them, and he started by lecturing on the subject of the Church from 1834 to 1836. In 1837 he gave a series on the theology of grace and justification. Over the period he continued his own studies of the Church of the early centuries, and had been writing a series of articles entitled 'Letters on the Church of the Fathers'. In September of 1837 he began planning with Pusey the monumental *Library of the Fathers*, a major collaborative effort by scholars to produce translations of patristic writings, the first volume to appear being Pusey's *Confessions of St Augustine* in 1838. That year too Newman reluctantly became editor of the *British Critic*, a monthly review, while continuing his work with the Tracts. Over the following three years, and under his careful editorship, the *British Critic* became the principal voice of the Movement.

In April 1837 he started an early Eucharist on Sunday mornings in St Mary's, which was the only weekly celebration in Oxford at that time, and was well attended. He also said daily Matins, although few came. And the regular rounds of his other duties as parish priest continued, with baptisms, weddings, burials. As always he was visiting the sick, especially out at Littlemore, and giving confirmation classes. And with much welcomed university students he began lively Monday evening gatherings, where the conversation was wide-ranging, and anything but religious. James Anthony Froude, younger brother of Hurrell, the later historian and agnostic, remembered attending those evenings long after, where their host was never didactic or authoritative: 'He was lightness itself – the lightness of elastic strength ...' 'Newman's mind was world-wide,' he wrote. 'He was interested in everything which was going on in science, in politics, in literature ... He could admire enthusiastically any greatness of action and character, however remote the sphere of it from his own.'

Also in 1837 his first series of Adam de Brome lectures was published as *The Prophetical Office of the Church*. There he laid out what he believed was a strong theological justification for the Church of England, portraying it as a middle way – a *Via Media* – between the extremes of Protestantism and Romanism. He and his followers were beginning to be criticised at that time as leaning towards the Church of Rome, and among other things he wished to rebut that charge by showing that the Anglican Church could legitimately claim to be a part of that ancient 'Church Catholic and Apostolic' which he loved, and which he saw as the template for any authentic contemporary Christian Church. He acknowledged the pain of disunity among Christians, and knew that the fragmentation had damaged the various traditions of Christendom. But he felt that his own Church in essence had remained faithful to, and by apostolical succession was linked to, the great Church of the early centuries. Protestantism in his mind tended to devalue or ignore the meaning of 'One Holy, Catholic and Apostolic' in the Creed, while the Roman Church had illegitimately added to and corrupted aspects of the great tradition it inherited.

The next year he published his *Lectures on Justification*, which treated the main originating controversy of the Reformation, between Lutherans and Catholics, on how we are redeemed from sin and changed by the grace of God in Christ. Again his method was scriptural and historical, through an analysis of the New Testament and examination of the Fathers. This enabled him to go beyond the polemic arguments of the sixteenth century, to outline in a clear manner the reality of grace as none other than the personal indwelling of God, which is Christ's presence within us, secured by the action of the Holy Spirit. In this utterly personal and divine way we are justified, and it is done principally through the sacraments of the Church, at Baptism, and intensified in Holy Communion.

He had already treated the subject over three years before, in the sermon 'The Indwelling Spirit'. And now in 'The Spiritual Presence of Christ in the Church', preached some months after the book's publication, he returned to it, speaking of the indwelling presence as personal to each, yet multiform throughout all believers who are united together as 'members of the Body of Christ'. We do not therefore just look towards Christ, for he is already within us, and 'takes possession of us as his purchased inheritance; He does not present himself to us, but he takes us to him. He makes us his members.'[7] Always, Newman's understanding of the Christian mysteries would be of that kind, as the forming of bonds between persons, human and divine. The secret of his own life, and his prayer, could be found there too.

He brought out the fourth volume of his *Parochial Sermons* towards the end of 1838, a collection of what he felt were some of the best he had written to date. It included 'The Ventures of Faith', preached nearly three years earlier. There, Newman said that the life of faith implies risking everything on Christ's word, without care for the future, but in all things leaning and waiting upon him. Yet that is what many, who call themselves Christian, will stop short of doing, whatever they may profess, or think, or feel. But it is what the disciples James and John meant when they said to Christ, 'We are able' (Mt 20:22). One of those listening to Newman when he preached on that occasion was the young Richard Church, who was so moved by what he heard that he resolved there and then to give his life to the Gospel and to its ministry.

Another sermon, 'The Invisible World', was preached originally in Cholderton, where Harriet's husband Tom Mozley had his living. In it, Newman treats with great formal beauty that theme central to him all his life, where he invites us to look by faith into the greater world surrounding and touching our own:

> And yet in spite of this universal world which we see, there is another world, quite as far-spreading, quite as close to us, and more wonderful; another world all around us, though we see it not, and more wonderful than the world we see, for this reason if for no other, that we do not see it … Once, and once only, for thirty-three years, has He condescended to become one of the beings which are seen, when He, the second Person of the

Ever-blessed Trinity, was, by an unspeakable mercy, born of the Virgin Mary into this sensible world ... He came, and He retired beyond the veil: and to us individually, it is as if He had never shown Himself; we have as little sensible experience of His presence. Yet 'He liveth evermore' ... The earth that we see does not satisfy us; it is but a beginning, it is but a promise of something beyond it ... A world of Saints and Angels, a glorious world, the palace of God, the mountain of the Lord of Hosts ... all these wonders, everlasting, all-precious, mysterious, and incomprehensible, lie hid in what we see. What we see is the outward shell of an eternal kingdom; and on that kingdom we fix the eyes of our faith.[8]

The same theme occurs in 'The Greatness and Littleness of Human Life', where there is a description of what is good in this life, but only seen as such when it leads to love of things invisible. Our own world, if left to itself, can only promise what it cannot accomplish. It is only precious 'as revealing to us, amid shadows and figures, the existence of Almighty God and his elect people'.

Finally, it may be remarked that three great texts in the volume focus on aspects of Christ's presence and our looking to him. An Advent sermon named 'Watching' makes out in detail from the New Testament how the Christian is characterised by an attitude of daily looking out for Christ in all things. 'This then is to watch; to be detached from what is present, and to live in what is unseen; to live in the thought of Christ as he came once, and as he will come again; to desire his second coming, from our affectionate and grateful remembrance of his first.' A sermon for Christmas Day 1837, 'Christ hidden from the World', stresses the emptying and poverty of Christ both at the Incarnation and now in the earthen vessel of the Church. 'He has made the poor, weak, and afflicted, tokens and instruments of his presence', but the great self-important world passes by without awareness of him, just as it did in the days of his flesh.

Then in 'Christ Manifested in Remembrance' it is remarked how events in life usually only reveal their meaning in retrospect, and that as far as God's ordinances are concerned, 'we do not discern them at the time, except by faith, afterwards only'. 'There is nothing of heaven in the face of society; in the news of the day there is nothing of heaven … And yet the Ever-blessed Spirit of God is here; the Presence of the Eternal Son, ten times more glorious, more powerful than when He trod the earth in our flesh, is with us.'

Much more could be said about the range and depth of Newman's preaching, and their extraordinary effect on listeners and readers. It is not an exaggeration to say that his sermons, especially his parochial ones, at this time and later, stand out as his greatest legacy from the years of the Oxford Movement. They represent what it stood for, as an invitation to a young receptive generation to reach up to the high truths of the Gospel, and through a recovered appreciation of the ancient but still living Catholic tradition. Newman had become very concerned with what he and others saw as a drift towards rationalism and Liberalism in religion. The affluent circumstances of many of his congregation and readers, the general confidence in progress, and the easy accommodation of much religion to these conditions all gave an urgency to his words. Rather like a prophet of old, he spoke out in opposition to what he saw as only a fashionable veneer of religious profession, the comfortable 'religion of the world' and of the 'self-wise'. In its place he presents a clear vision of the real truths and moral implications of Catholic Christianity, so that consciences might be awakened, and people might hear once again the perennial Gospel call to venture all on the person and teachings of Christ, relying on his grace given in the Church. And what he set out then, in essence, would never change in the rest of his life, although it would be complemented and enriched in certain respects. The spirit of Newman is uniquely present in the words spoken in St Mary's, giving the key to what he would always live by, and offer to others, in all the winding and sometimes very unexpected circumstances of his later Catholic life.

NOTES

1. *Apo*, p. 39.
2. Ibid., p. 61.
3. Richard Church, *The Oxford Movement: Twelve Years 1833–1845*, London: Macmillan, 1891, p. 113.
4. Ibid., p. 168.
5. cf. *PS*, I, pp. 309–24.
6. *LD*, V, p. 32.
7. *PS*, VI, p. 121.
8. *PS*, IV, pp. 201–3, 210–11.

— CHAPTER 3 —

'A Great Revolution of Mind'

I T WAS CLEAR, however, that Newman and his companions in the Oxford Movement were leaving themselves open to the charge of leaning towards Rome. Although the Creed might speak of 'One, Holy, Catholic and Apostolic', and the Tractarians in their publications would say they were only recovering for their generation aspects of that Catholic consciousness which had been forgotten, there was an innate Protestant suspicion about what they portrayed. The Evangelical side of the Church was suspicious above all, but so too were many middle-ground Anglicans, as well as the more Liberally-minded.

In 1838 Newman, in association with Keble, published *Remains of Richard Hurrell Froude*. Extracts from his private journal and letters, *Remains* revealed the extent of Froude's rejection of the Reformation and his love of Catholic truth, as well as his life of prayer and self-discipline. Many were alarmed by the publication, and were roused to increase their opposition to the Movement. In addition, the Bishop of Oxford expressed some concern about the continuing Tracts – but when in deference to him Newman offered to cease publication, the mild Dr Bagot, who was himself a High Churchman, said nothing as definite as that needed to be done. Again, when a translation of the Roman Breviary was mooted, which he was using regularly, there was opposition among some of Newman's acquaintances, and the idea was dropped.

Then came the year 1839, when matters began to change for him personally, and irrevocably, bringing him along 'the course of that great revolution of mind, which led me to leave my own home, to which I was bound by so many strong and tender ties.'[1] In that springtime, as the *Apologia* relates, 'my position in the Anglican Church was at its height. I had supreme confidence in my controversial *status*, and I had a great and still growing success, in recommending it to others.'[2] The Movement was a force throughout the world of Anglicanism, with his well-argued *Via Media* theory providing what seemed a real and substantive justification for the Church's existence, grounding it in the Catholicism of antiquity, and in the patristic theology of the seventeenth-century divines, and buttressing it against the Liberal onslaughts of the day.

But during the summer holidays Newman was struck by a doubt about his view of Anglicanism, as a result of an extensive study he was making of the Church in the fifth century. He saw how at that time continuing controversy over Christology had led Pope Leo the Great to call the Council of Chalcedon (451), which voted to condemn the Monophysite view of Christ, held by both the extreme group of Eutyches and by the more moderate Eastern Church. In both of these areas of Monophysitism, deemed to be heretical, Newman was shocked to see the possible equivalent of Protestantism and Anglicanism respectively. As he said later, 'My stronghold was Antiquity; now here, in the middle of the fifth century, I found, as it seemed to me, the Christendom of the sixteenth and the nineteenth centuries reflected. I saw my face in that mirror, and I was a Monophysite. The Church of the *Via Media* was in the position of the Oriental communion, Rome was where she now is; and the Protestants were the Eutychians.'[3] In addition, he was impressed by the authority Pope Leo the Great claimed over East and West, and how he based his position upon St Peter. It was as if the Pope's jurisdiction then was the same as that claimed by contemporary Rome.

He had a further cause for worry when in September a friend asked him to read an article by Nicholas Wiseman in the *Dublin Review*, a Catholic quarterly recently founded by him, on the

'Anglican Claim to Apostolical Succession'. Wiseman there drew a parallel between the Anglicans and the schismatic Donatists of North Africa. He demonstrated how St Augustine, in the midst of that local controversy, found against the Donatists by appealing to the general consent of Christendom. Augustine's phrase was '*Securus judicat orbis terrarum*', which was translated by Wiseman as 'Wherefore, the entire world judges with security, that they are not good, who separate themselves from the entire world, in whatever part of the world.' At first Newman did not feel the force of Augustine's words. But his friend kept repeating them, and then he was stunned – struck with a power that he had never felt from any words before.[4] '*Securus judicat orbis terrarum.*' Was the Anglican communion after all, despite its appeal to antiquity, cut off by the acts of the English Reformation and the Elizabethan Settlement from 'the entire world' of Christendom? And was that 'entire world' now as in the past centred on Rome?

It was like seeing a ghost, but only momentarily. 'The heavens had opened and closed again.' For that instant the thought had been, 'The Church of Rome will be found right after all.'[5] But then the doubts seemed to vanish, and he roused himself to defend his Church. Soon after he preached the sermon 'Divine Calls', which has much on how God never ceases to call us onward, throughout all the events of our lives, and ends with an exhortation to 'pray Him day by day, to reveal himself to our souls more fully'.[6] He also wrote an article for the *British Critic* in answer to Wiseman, and concluded that, 'In spite of our being separated from Greece and Rome, shut up in ourselves and our dependencies, and looked coldly at and forgotten by the rest of Christendom, there is sufficient ground for still believing that the English Church is at this time the Catholic Church in England.'

Through the following winter, life continued much as before. In March 1840 he published *The Church of the Fathers*, a reworked collection of the articles he had written from 1833 onwards under the same general title. There, the early Christian world in East and West was shown as relevant for contemporary Church life, and especially by the vivid portrayal of figures such as Ambrose, Basil, Gregory Nazianzen, Augustine, Antony, and Martin of Tours. An attractive ideal of holiness was put forward in the book, and which was to have wide influence. Later in the year the fifth volume of *Parochial Sermons* appeared. It contains the sermon 'Unreal Words', which in its way highlights something Newman feared most, namely the instances in the Church 'when love has waxed cold and faith failed,'[7] its inner life being eaten out, and the professions of its adherents hollow and unreal. Other notable sermons included are 'Equanimity' and 'The Thought of God the Stay of the Soul'.

During Lent 1840 Newman went out to stay alone at Littlemore, taking lodgings there, and with a view to helping out in any way he could. The opportunity presented itself because of a change of curates, with an interval in between, Bloxam having resigned to look after his ill father and William Copeland about to come as a replacement. Personally Newman wished to fast and pray there. He had already been fasting in Lent for a number of years, but now he did so more severely and especially through Holy Week. And he prayed the full office of the Breviary every day. At times he missed the company of friends, some of whom through marriage were not now so close, while others in any case had simply moved on from Oxford. Not that he was unaware of the suffering which could come the way of families, as in the loss to a heartbroken Pusey of his wife Maria the previous year, which had been preceded by the death of their young daughter Katherine. The Pusey household had been almost a second home for him. He nevertheless remained convinced of his own single calling, and indeed in the *Church of the Fathers* had highlighted the value placed on celibacy in earlier times. But he had just now entered his fortieth year, and felt in an acute way the loss of the sympathy and interest married life offered. He wrote in his notebook: 'I willingly give up the possession of that sympathy, which I feel is not, and cannot be, granted to me. Yet, not the less do I feel the need of it … Shall I ever have in my old age spiritual children who will take an interest such as a wife does?'[8]

Musings aside, he was writing in lively fashion to Jemima, who had known everyone in Littlemore and all the goings-on. He found that much needed to be done in the poor school that had been started there. On the girls' side, he noticed quite a degree of neglect, and tracked down the cause to a weakness for drink in 'Mrs W', the schoolmistress. He had to set about remedying the situation. Then taking out an old violin, he started up a choir 'of between twenty and thirty great and little in the schoolroom'. Also he drew up 'a sort of Liturgy for School Prayers, varying with the seasons'. In addition, on Sundays he gathered some children in the church to teach them their faith. The theologian James Mozley, another of his sisters' family, wrote home: 'Newman's catechising has been the great attraction this Lent, and men have gone out of Oxford every Sunday to hear it. I thought it very striking, done with such spirit, and the children so up to it.' And Easter Sunday itself crowned it all, Bloxam having turned up the previous evening to help out. They put on an altar cloth made by Jemima and the Mozleys in Derby, and got 'some roses, wallflowers and sweet-briar'. The girls especially were looking their best, in pink bonnets and white pinafores, and the choir in top form singing the Psalms in the Gregorian chant he had taught them.

It was a lovely time. Oxford by contrast was impersonal, and the thought was crossing his mind to possibly leave St Mary's and stay permanently at Littlemore. But the advice he got, especially from Keble, was to keep going and not act precipitously. There was still much to engage his energies in that wider and increasingly controversial world – and soon the amount of controversy would be fiercer and more sustained than anything he could have imagined.

Early in 1841 he was asked by the editor of *The Times* to write a series of articles for the newspaper, to comment on an important speech by Sir Robert Peel, leader of the Conservative Party. At the opening of a reading room in Tamworth, Peel had put forward a quite utilitarian view of education, implying that improved education for the masses rather than religion would be the best means of making people more virtuous. Newman wrote anonymously for the paper seven 'Letters of Catholicus', wittily debunking Peel's belief that the diffusion of useful knowledge would lead to moral improvement. He was not against the widening of opportunities for education and practical knowledge, but against the widespread utilitarian philosophy often accompanying it, that it could be a substitute for religious belief. 'Who was ever consoled in real trouble by the small beer of literature or science?' he asked. 'You must go to a higher source for renovation of the heart and will.'

But of course the Roman question kept coming up. Others had read Wiseman's article, and were unsettled. The very Catholic ideals that the Tractarians espoused were in themselves turning people to look towards Rome. Newman was acutely aware of this, and felt a responsibility to keep them in the Church he served. For years he had been considering a treatment of the Thirty-Nine Articles, the formularies of Anglicanism since early Elizabethan times, with a view to bringing out what he believed was their underlying Catholic meaning. This would not be easy. While the Prayer Book contained much of the treasury from a Catholic past, the ethos of the Articles was more clearly Protestant, and in places they were aimed against Roman doctrines and practices. Newman himself disliked the Protestant tone of the Articles, and yet he was bound to them. But he believed that he could show, in concert with some of the seventeenth-century Caroline divines, that they were not in fundamental opposition to the ancient Catholic teachings. In doing this, he might prevent people from joining the Roman Church, which too had allowed distortions into its teaching and into the life of its members. He would help those wishing for a deeper faith to appreciate that their own English communion, whatever its imperfections, was a true and worthy branch of the one enduring Catholic Church.

His treatment, which was of fourteen of the Thirty-Nine Articles, came out anonymously on 27 February 1841 as the famous *Tract 90*. It was to be the last of the *Tracts for the Times*. To use the word in its more modern sense, it was 'ecumenical' in its purpose, desiring to show there was a common ground inhabited by Anglicanism and Rome. He followed the Articles in their condemnation of the old Roman practical teachings on such as Purgatory, indulgences, the honouring of images and relics, the invocation of the saints, the sacraments, transubstantiation, the sacrificial aspect of the Mass, and the power of the Pope. But it was the pre-Tridentine exaggerations the Articles addressed, and not the teaching and practices modified by the Council of Trent, and which could be acceptable to a degree. Matters had moved on since the Articles were framed originally. On his own side, he acknowledged that Anglicanism could be prone to the weaknesses of a fundamentally anti-Catholic Protestantism. It needed to appropriate its Catholic heritage more fully, and also be prepared to admit the essential Catholicity of Rome. It would be good if both sides could confess their sinfulness and aberrations, born of pride and power, and instead display humble repentance and greater reliance on the Gospel.

Already the anonymous 'Letters of Catholicus' against Peel had caused a good deal of excitement, with various Liberal attacks being made on 'Puseyism', including in the House of Lords. But a real storm was set off by the publication of *Tract 90*, both in Oxford and across the country, and for which Newman was unprepared. Soon he had to publicly acknowledge that he was the author. Following on from a vote of censure by the Heads of Houses, and flooded with letters from furious Evangelicals, Bishop Bagot let it be known that he too objected to Newman's interpretation of the Articles. This time he would insist on ending the Tracts. Newman took seriously his Bishop's views, and there was a correspondence between them. The outcome was Newman's agreement to end the Tracts, while the Bishop – courteous as always in his dealings with Newman – would allow *Tract 90* to stand. In this way it was hoped to avoid condemnation from the wider body of bishops.

But there continued a chorus of indignation, both from the Evangelical side of the Church and from the Liberals. The fact was he had hit a nerve in the national psyche. While a thoughtful few could appreciate his endeavours, the great majority could not and would not, and were up in arms. The Thirty-Nine Articles were somehow tied in with the identity of the nation, and that identity was an historic Protestant one. Much of public opinion went against Newman therefore, and in consequence the bishops too. Despite his agreement with Bishop Bagot, gradually over the next three years virtually all of the bishops across the land would condemn *Tract 90*. Their condemnations, in what were known as their triennial Charges, would be a slow and cumulative process. But already, from the early reactions to *Tract 90*, it was clear that Newman had lost the leadership of the Oxford Movement.

Again in Lent of that year he took board and lodging out at Littlemore, although he was often found to be back in Oxford. Keble and Pusey remained his best supports, Keble having seen and agreed with *Tract 90* before publication, and Pusey at all times afterwards stoutly defending it and its author. On Good Friday he preached in St Mary's one of his most memorable sermons, 'The Cross of Christ the Measure of the World':

> It is the death of the eternal Word of God made flesh, which is our great lesson how to think and how to speak of this world. His Cross has put its due value upon everything which we see, upon all fortune, all advantages, all ranks, all dignities ... It has taught us how to live, how to use this world, what to expect, what to desire, what to hope ... Thus in the Cross, and Him who hung upon it, all things meet; all things subserve it, all things need it. It is their centre and their interpretation. For He was lifted upon it, that He might draw all men and all things unto Him.[9]

In the summer of 1841 he moved out to Littlemore again. At the same time he resigned the editorship of the *British Critic*, as he had intended to do for some time, handing it over to his brother-in-law Tom Mozley. He became busy in translating the anti-Arian treatises of St Athanasius for the *Library of the Fathers* – and here he found himself making another parallel with the present, the Arian parties being the equivalent of the Protestants and the Anglicans, and Rome in the same position then as now. 'The ghost had come a second time.' In the autumn, he was disturbed further when a plan was announced that a joint Anglican-Lutheran bishopric would be set up in Jerusalem, the bishops to be alternately appointed by England and by Prussia. It was a projected move unashamedly Protestant in character, and offensively so, being an encroachment upon the Eastern Catholic Churches, Greek and Latin. He wrote a searing letter of protest to Bishop Bagot and to Archbishop Howley of Canterbury.

During Advent he preached four sermons in St Mary's, in which he was anxious to steady those unsettled by the recent events. In 'The

Invisible Presence of Christ', while acknowledging the confusion and disorder in the Church, he asked his hearers to depend upon the personal tokens of grace which were still evident to them – 'if your soul has been, as it were, transfigured within you, when you came to the Most Holy Sacrament; or if Lent and Passiontide brought to you what you had not before ... O! pause ere you doubt that we have a Divine Presence among us still, and have not to seek it. Let us enjoy what we still have, though the world deride us.' In a similar vein he preached 'Outward and Inward Notes of the Church' and 'Grounds for Steadfastness in Our Religious Profession', pointing to the hidden but real examples of grace people had experienced personally in the Church. Then, in 'Elijah the Prophet of the Latter Days' he made a comparison between the separated northern kingdom of Samaria in Elijah's time and the position of his own Church. Despite its schism from Judah and the Temple in Jerusalem, Elijah was still called solely to minister in that hapless kingdom. And when he had to flee for his life, Elijah passed by Jerusalem, 'along a forlorn and barren way', returning to Horeb, the mountain of God. 'He fled to antiquity, and would not stop short of it, and so he heard the words of comfort which reconciled him to his work and to its issue.'[10] Newman was still, as best as he could, finding grounds for himself and others to stay within the fold of the Anglican Church. And that portrayal of Elijah bore more than a passing resemblance to his own story and present dark situation.

Meanwhile, a gradual process of withdrawal from Oxford was taking place. At Littlemore Newman obtained the lease of some 'L-shaped cottages', which had been used recently as a stable for the Oxford-Cambridge coach. They 'consisted of a barn, a stable or two and a few mean cottages, giving on to the yard'. In early February 1842 all his books were on the move from Oriel, to be set up in the barn. The cottages were being converted into simple living quarters for himself and for whoever else might choose to stay. Jemima was anxious for him, and he had to write a reassuring letter to her, saying that for some years he had felt out of place at Oxford, being now one of the more senior people there. Yes, he did admit there was official hostility to him, so that he was thinking of giving up preaching. 'I think my preaching is a cause of *irritation*, and, for what I know, any moment they may do something against me at St Mary's, and I would rather anticipate this.'

He moved into his new abode after Easter, and soon there were rumours, and a newspaper report that 'a so-called Anglo-Catholic monastery' was being established. Newman in consequence had to defend himself to the Bishop, saying that for years he had wanted to lead 'a life of greater religious regularity', and would expect others living there to be involved 'in study and in joint devotion'. Soon he had a 'small household', which included his curate Copeland. Also there was John Dobree Dalgairns, from Guernsey in the Channel Islands, who would go on be an Oratorian, and under Newman for a time. Later in the summer the place was full – but 'men come and go; I have hardly one constant inmate, and in winter perhaps I may be left alone'. Generally, those who came were young men searching for that Catholic way of life expounded by Newman and the Tractarians over the past few years, and which their Church was now seemingly against. Some were recommended to Newman by their families in the hope that he would dissuade them from 'going over to Rome'. They formed a community of sorts, doing their own housework, having regular prayer together, and simple after-dinner recreation.

In the wake of the reaction to *Tract 90*, a variety of people whose lives had been enriched by the Oxford Movement were beginning to despair of the Anglican Church. They now more seriously thought of converting to Rome, to join the small number who had already 'gone over'. This was a great worry to Newman. He knew his own leadership and influence had much to do with where they found themselves now. He felt a responsibility for them, to keep them from seceding. Yet he himself was in an acute dilemma, being more and more subject to thoughts that the Roman claims were plausible, although he felt in conscience he must treat such thoughts as temptations. He shared what was going on in himself with very few, and the thought continued to recur that he might have to withdraw from St Mary's at some opportune time. Meanwhile he had to help the young men who came his way at Littlemore, and also to respond to the many enquirers high and low who wrote seeking advice from him.

Among those in contact with him was Mary Holmes, a governess at that time, who had become a Tractarian. Their correspondence would last her lifetime, for some thirty-eight years, until 1878. Another was Emily Bowles, whose friendship with him would extend to the end of his own life, and to whom Newman on occasion would write very freely and personally. Equally close to him now and throughout her life would be Catherine Froude (née Holdsworth), married to Hurrell's engineer brother William. And he was also writing regularly, as he would always do, to Maria Giberne, helping to steady her by faith in God's continuing providence.

Some Roman Catholics came his way as well, although he felt ill at ease in his dealings with them, considering it his duty to keep at a distance. An exception was with Dr Charles Russell, an Irish priest ten years his junior, who was Professor of Humanity at Maynooth College and co-editor with Wiseman of the *Dublin Review*. Russell had been following the Oxford Movement with interest, and after the publication of *Tract 90* started a correspondence with Newman. Despite their disagreements, their letters show that at heart they shared in a deep love of the Eucharist.[11] Newman grew to respect him, and to feel a warmth towards him that was absent in his contacts with the other Roman Catholics. They would meet in person in Oxford on 1 August 1843. In the *Apologia* he would write that Russell 'had, perhaps, more to do with my conversion than any one else … he was always gentle, mild, unobtrusive, uncontroversial. He let me alone.'[12]

In 1842 there appeared the first part of his translations of the *Select Treatises of S. Athanasius, Archbishop of Alexandria, in Controversy with the Arians*. Much work had gone into its making, eight to twelve hours a day sustained for long periods. If Elijah in the schismatic northern kingdom of Israel may be considered a hero for Newman, much more so was Athanasius, the great unwavering fourth-century champion of Catholic Nicene orthodoxy, who along with the lay faithful held the Church steady in its faith, despite large numbers of bishops falling away, and the vacillating weak Pope Liberius.

This year too Newman completed the set of *Parochial Sermons* with a sixth volume, the selection arranged to cover the Church cycle from

Lent through Easter and to Trinity. It included 'The Cross of Christ the Measure of the World'. Other significant titles to be found in it were 'The Spiritual Presence of Christ in the Church', noted earlier, as well as 'The Eucharistic Presence', 'Warfare the Condition of Victory', 'Waiting for Christ', 'The Weapons of Saints', 'The Mystery of the Holy Trinity', and 'Peace in Believing'. The sermon 'Divine Calls', however, was soon to be placed in a separate collection of his, entitled *Plain Sermons*, which was part of a series made up of the offerings of various Tractarian authors.

His valuable collection of *University Sermons* was published in February 1843. Although these were delivered in two separate periods of time, they nevertheless are related, in their examination of various aspects of faith and reason. The 1830–1832 group of sermons, as noted already, were attempts to work out a philosophy of religion. After these is placed the sermon 'Wilfulness, the Sin of Saul', preached just before setting out on the fateful Mediterranean journey. The next five were delivered much later, between 1839 and 1841, and form a close-knit unity, even though spread out in time, with consecutive ones reiterating previous themes as well as introducing new material. Some of Newman's very best thought is here, perhaps especially in two preached close together, 'Faith and Reason, Contrasted as Habits of Mind' and 'The Nature of Faith in Relation to Reason'. The processes of our mind, both in reasoning and in evaluating things, and also in reaching towards faith, are explored with great insight and suppleness. The evidences for faith in the world are evaluated, and the need for revealed religion. Faith is seen as itself reasonable, yet reaching beyond what reason can attain. The place of love, and the heart, and conscience, are highlighted. Perhaps rarely have these issues been explored and delineated with such living reality as in Newman here. Later, he would revisit this whole field in the *Grammar of Assent*. As well, in 'Wisdom, as Contrasted with Faith and with Bigotry', there is a foretaste of his understanding of the enlargement of mind which would be described in *The Idea of a University*.

The concluding sermon, 'The Theory of Developments in Religious Doctrine', he had prepared in haste and delivered shortly before the publication of the book. Again, it is a seminal outline of what was already engaging him and would occupy him at the very end of his Anglican life. Were the great Catholic doctrinal statements or dogmas a superfluous superstructure on biblical Christian faith? And were other teachings such as that of Purgatory illegitimate additions, leading to corruptions in worship and prayer? Newman wished to show that there were in fact authentic developments over the centuries in Catholic Christian understanding, and he wanted to outline theologically how such growth could take place. He took as his text 'Mary kept all these things, and pondered them in her heart'. He saw the Church's reflection and arrival at definitions as being in the spirit of Mary's pondering. And he admitted that proper Catholic definitions and dogmas did not exhaust in any sense the Divine mystery they spoke of, but instead respected the mystery. Clearly, with views such as these, the die was being cast, with the increasing prospect of severance at some stage from the Church he served and loved.

NOTES

1. *Apo*, p. 92.
2. Ibid., p. 93.
3. *Apo*, p. 114.
4. cf. ibid., p. 117.
5. Ibid., p. 118.
6. *PS*, VIII, p. 32.
7. *PS*, V, p. 41.
8. *AW*, pp. 137–8.
9. *PS*, VI, pp. 84–6.
10. *SD*, p. 376.
11. cf. *LD*, VIII, pp. 171–5, 180–3, 186–8.
12. *Apo*, p. 194.

— CHAPTER 4 —

The Parting of Friends

IN THIS EARLY part of 1843, Newman was more convinced that his long association with St Mary's would have to come to an end. He had continued to share his concerns on the matter especially with Keble. Also at this time he quietly brought out a 'Retraction of Anti-Catholic Statements'. He was conscious of the anti-Roman polemic in some of his earlier writings, including in Tracts he had written, often when he felt he should vigorously defend the Anglican position. Now that he felt differently to an extent, he thought it only fair to issue the retraction. But as he wrote to a friend, he was despondent at doing it, because he would like 'to be out of hot water, and something or other is always sousing me again in it'.

Soon another Lent was upon the group at Littlemore, all accommodation there being taken up. Already Newman had read a life of St Ignatius Loyola, and had been struck by the holiness of the Roman saints '*since* our separation', especially the Jesuits. Now he was immersing himself in the text of the *Spiritual Exercises* of Ignatius, and would make detailed notes from the recent Latin critical edition, with official directories attached, by Ignatio Diertins SJ. He also made notes from Rosmini's *Manual for Retreats*, passed to him from Father Luigi Gentili, the saintly head of the Rosminians in England. Again it was a Lent of fasting and prayer, and using the hours of the Breviary. For the first five weeks Newman and his companions had an hour's meditation together each morning before Matins, using works of devotion by two seventeenth-century continental Catholic authors. Then for Holy Week they made as best they could an Ignatian retreat, taking the central themes of the Exercises, and spending Good Friday on the Passion. A help for them was a book just published, *Meditations and Considerations for a Spiritual Retreat of Eight Days*, by the late Marmaduke Stone SJ of Stonyhurst College. They would have wished to have a director, but had none, '*because*', as Newman later told a friend of his, James Hope, 'we did not know where to go for one'.

One of his sermons in St Mary's afterwards, preached during Eastertide and entitled 'The Shepherd of our Souls', outlined the scriptural teaching of Christ as the Good Shepherd, and stressed the need to look to him alone for light and guidance. His words were surely apt for himself and others of his followers at that time:

> Let us not be content with ourselves; let us not make our own hearts our home; let us look out for a better country, that is, a heavenly. Let us look out for Him who alone can guide us to that better country; let us call heaven our home, and this life a pilgrimage; let us view ourselves, as sheep in the trackless desert, who, unless they follow the shepherd, will be sure to lose themselves … We are safe while we keep close to Him, and under His eye … [1]

In the summer there was a significant addition to Littlemore's community, when Ambrose St John arrived, who had been curate to Newman's friend Henry Wilberforce, who himself had taken orders and married in 1834. Aged twenty-eight, Ambrose St John was mature and practical, and a good linguist. He would spend the rest of his life with Newman, and be an incalculable support. But while some younger friends came his way, other older and closer ones he had known would depart from him, such as his former pupil Frederic Rogers. They were drawing back from him because he ventured to acknowledge to them his Roman leanings. There were of course some, like the Tractarian lawyer James Hope, whom he had known since 1837, who would continue to be close to him. James Hope was one of those disillusioned over the reaction to *Tract 90* and the Jerusalem bishopric, and who would depart from Anglicanism. He was a friend of Henry Edward Manning, who had some acquaintance with Newman, and William Gladstone, who as an undergraduate had been a follower of Newman's sermons in St Mary's. Both Manning, as a Catholic prelate, and Gladstone, in his political career, who remained firm in his High Church Anglican faith, would feature prominently in Newman's life later on.

Later this year Newman's relationship with his sister Harriet was broken. Momentarily her impulsive husband Tom had thought of becoming a Roman Catholic, and Harriet, mistakenly believing her brother was the cause, could not forgive him. But as he pondered his future, Jemima by contrast still tried to support him: '... whichever way you decide,' she wrote, 'it will be a noble and true part, and not taken up from any impulse, or caprice, or pique, but on true and right principles that will carry a blessing with them.'[2] Yet, when he gradually grew closer to Rome, in her continuing love for him she could only experience pain and bewilderment.

By now, nearly all of the triennial bishops' Charges since *Tract 90* had been published, and were unanimously against his Catholic interpretation of the Thirty-Nine Articles. It was clear now what course of action he would have to take. In early September he finally acted on St Mary's, and sent in his resignation of its living to his Bishop. He had informed Dr Bagot before of the step he intended to take, and so he commented: '... it is not surprising that I should be determined on it now, when so many Bishops have said such things of me, and no one has taken my part in respect to that interpretation of the articles under which alone I can subscribe to them.'[3] On Sunday 24 September 1843 he preached as vicar in St Mary's for the last time. Up to the very end he had been keeping up his varied parish duties, and just then completed a series of confirmation classes.

In the church at Littlemore the next day, which was celebrating the anniversary of its consecration, he preached his final Anglican sermon, 'The Parting of Friends'. He took the text of his very first sermon many years before: 'Man goeth forth to his work and to his labour until the evening.' It was during the communion service, with

Pusey officiating, and in tears. The church was again decorated, this time with dahlias, passion-flowers and fuchsias. All the children were there, beautifully turned out in their frocks and bonnets, Newman's last gift to them, and their choir chanting a psalm in procession before the large congregation, which overflowed into the churchyard outside. He now retired into lay communion.

Although two more years were to elapse before Newman made his transition to the Church of Rome, there is perhaps little to relate. In the *Apologia* he would say later that from 1841 he was on his 'death-bed' regarding membership of the Anglican Church: 'A death-bed has scarcely a history; it is a tedious decline, with seasons of rallying and seasons of falling back; and since the end is foreseen, or what is called a matter of time, it has little interest for the reader, especially if he has a kind heart.'[4] Certainly, he was gone now from the public scenes of controversy. Life went on quietly at Littlemore, with much prayer and study. People came and went. Some of them, and others in different places who had been inspired by him, were determining to leave Anglicanism and become Roman Catholics. He felt deeply the distress and confusion his situation was causing. Even with an increasing sense that he must one day submit to Rome, he was haunted by the fear that he could be under an illusion. He shared his thoughts and feelings intimately with Keble – but he, like Pusey, resolving not to leave the Anglican Church, could be of little help.

Sermons on Subjects of the Day came out in late 1843, dedicated to William Copeland, 'the kindest of friends', who continued to look after Littlemore. It included the 1841 Advent sermons which, uncharacteristically for Newman, stressed religious experience, looking at personal tokens of grace as indicators of Christ's continuing presence in the English Church. At the end of the volume is, appropriately, the Littlemore sermon 'The Parting of Friends'. And one other sermon in the collection, 'Wisdom and Innocence', treating of the Gospel's sending forth of the disciples, as sheep in the midst of wolves (Mt 10:16), has concluding words which have remained familiar:

May He, as of old, choose 'the foolish things of the world to confound the wise, and the weak things of the world to confound the things which are mighty!' May He support us all the day long, till the shades lengthen, and the evening comes, and the busy world is hushed, and the fever of life is over, and our work is done! Then in His mercy may He give us a safe lodging, and a holy rest, and peace at the last![5]

Perhaps those words were remembered, with heartfelt meaning, over a year after they were uttered. For in April 1844 another of Pusey's daughters, Lucy, was dying, aged just fifteen. She had been intending to live a simple and single life, devoted to the poor. Pusey wrote to Newman, who had so greatly consoled him at the deaths of little Katherine and of his wife Maria. 'She is a child of your writings,' he said, and reported Lucy's words to be passed to Newman: 'Give him my respectful love, and thank him for all his kindness to me.' Newman wrote in reply:

> She was given you to be an heir of Heaven. Have you not been allowed to perform that part towards her? You have done your work – what remains but to present it finished to Him who put it upon you? ... How fitly do her so touching words which you report to me accord with such thoughts as these! ... Dear Lucy has been made His by Baptism, she has been made His in suffering; and now she asks to be made His by love ... Should you have a fit time for doing so, pray tell her that she is constantly in my thoughts, and will not, (so be it!) cease to be; – as she, who has gone first, is in my mind day by day, morning and evening, continually.[6]

Nearly two weeks later, on 22 April, Lucy died, her father often in the night having uttered with her the *Anima Christi* prayer, 'Soul of Christ'. Newman believed she was a saint, and ever after, as a Catholic priest, remembered her name daily, along with his own mother's before beginning Mass.

He continued to pray earnestly, looking for light and guidance. John Keble, hidden away in his country parish, received many letters from him, where Newman shared what was going on in his soul. This lovable, modest and quiet man, very aware of his own shortcomings, was the one Newman trusted above all. Towards the end of a long letter to him in June, he wrote as follows:

> What then is the will of Providence about me? The time for argument is passed. I have been in one settled conviction for so long a time, which every new thought seems to strengthen. When I fall in with friends who think differently, the temptation to remain quiet becomes stronger, very strong – but I really do not think my conviction is a bit shaken. So then I end as I began – Am I in delusion, given over to believe a lie? Am I deceiving myself convinced when I am not? Does any subtle meaning or temptation, which I cannot detect, govern me, and bias my judgment? – But is it possible that Divine Mercy should not wish me, if so, to discover and escape it? Has He led me thus far to destroy me in the wilderness? … How this letter will distress you! I am ever thinking of you, My dear Keble, Yrs affly JHN.[7]

That year too his first and dearest Oxford friend, John Bowden, was slowly dying from consumption, and Newman frequently travelled on the new Great Western rail routes, to Bristol and latterly to London, to see him, and to give him Holy Communion. Bowden died on 15 September 1844, his wife Elizabeth and the children round him, all supported by the strength of their faith. Elizabeth had promised him she would be guided by Newman, and in the event she was very glad of his continuing friendship and his interest in the children.

In November a false report appeared in the newspapers that he had already been received by Rome. In consequence he was inundated by letters, some very hostile, and many expressing confusion and pain. It was extremely difficult for him to receive these, and deal with the 'unsettling of so many peaceable, innocent minds'. However, early in 1845 he was unconcerned when the university moved to get Convocation to make a formal censure of

Tract 90. In the end Convocation failed in its effort, although it successfully condemned the pro-Roman book *Ideal of a Christian Church* by William George Ward, and deprived him of his degrees. Ward was a fiery Tractarian whose provocative views, disapproved of by Newman, were first aired in the *British Critic*, under the indulgent editorship of Tom Mozley.

Meanwhile he had decided to take up again the idea of doctrinal development, broached in his last university sermon, and work it out more fully. Tired as he was, he first completed the second part of his edition of St Athanasius, and then set about his new book, standing at his upright desk, and with vast materials to hand. It was to lead him to his final break with Protestantism – for that is now what he considered his Anglicanism to have been – and to embrace what he would no longer call the 'Roman Church' but simply the Catholic Church. Protestantism after all had in it a determination 'of dispensing with historical Christianity altogether, and of forming a Christianity from the Bible alone'.[8] It tended to ignore the long evolution of Christian history, and act as if it was just a stone's throw from New Testament times. But Catholicism was rooted in historical reality. It saw itself as an organic movement, certainly based on the immediacy of the New Testament, but continuing through history in the Church's teaching and sacraments, with an active centre of unity, all the time reaching back to the great moments which defined its understanding of God's action in Christ, and enabling it here and now to embody and to proclaim the living Christian mystery of salvation for the world.

As for Catholic Christian thought, or theology, he saw it as an assemblage of vital *ideas*, changing through time, while remaining true to themselves. They cannot be static, but must *develop*, because such is the way of human growth and history. 'In a higher world it is otherwise, but here below to live is to change, and to be perfect is to have changed often.'[9] Moreover, as a universal religion, Christianity had to adapt itself to different historical eras and places: '… it cannot but vary in its relations and dealings towards the world around it, that is, it will develop … Hence all bodies of Christians, orthodox or not, develop the doctrines of Scripture.'[10]

In the past he had appealed to Antiquity, to the Church of the Fathers, as the source and guarantee of Catholic truth. Now however it was very clear to him that more was required. History had continued since that privileged age, which in a special way drew on God's revelation given in Christ. But God's living revelation, once given, and then in part set out in particular epochal conciliar definitions, required a continuing authority for its proclamation over the ages.

> If Christianity is both social and dogmatic, and intended for all ages, it must, humanly speaking, have an infallible expounder. Else you will secure unity of form at the loss of unity of doctrine, or unity of doctrine at the loss of unity of form; you will have to choose between a comprehension of opinions and a resolution into parties, between latitudinarian and sectarian error. You may be tolerant or intolerant of contrarieties of thought, but contrarieties you will have.[11]

The Church therefore must have this centre of unity and authority. Newman now could see that this central authority actually resided in the contemporary Catholic and Roman Church, in the Holy See, and that this was what helped it to be in living and unbroken continuity with the Church of the Fathers. He went ahead with his densely argued material, full of historical examples of Catholic development, linked to an unchanging essential fidelity to the Gospel. Later published as *An Essay on the Development of Christian Doctrine*, the book would prove to be one of the most valuable and seminal theological works of modern times, although in the end never completed. For all at once Newman's residual doubts finally disappeared. He stopped writing, knowing there was nothing now left to do but prepare for the actual step of entry into the Church of Rome.

Matters were coming to a head in his little Littlemore community. On 29 September Dalgairns, who had travelled up to Stone in Staffordshire, was received into the Catholic Church by the Italian Passionist Fr Dominic Barberi. On 2 October Ambrose St John was received at Prior Park, near Bath. The next day Newman wrote to Provost Hawkins to resign his Oriel Fellowship. A few days later he heard that Fr Dominic would be passing by and paying a visit to Dalgairns. Newman had already met him, and felt he was a man of true holiness. So as Dalgairns went to meet the coach Newman asked him quietly: 'When you see your friend, will you tell him that I wish him to receive me into the Church of Christ?' It was late and pouring rain when Fr Dominic arrived, and as he was drying himself by the fire Newman came in and, kneeling down, asked him to hear his confession and receive him into the Church. He began his confession there, and in the morning continued. Fr Dominic then had to break off to go and say Mass in the Catholic Chapel in St Clement's, and to inform Mr Newsham, the Jesuit in residence there, about what was happening. Having returned in the still pouring rain he heard out the rest of Newman's confession. It was 9 October, 1845. That evening Newman, together with recent young companions who had joined him, Frederick Bowles (Emily's brother) and Richard Stanton, made their profession of faith and were given conditional Baptism. And the following morning Fr Dominic said Mass in their tiny chapel.

It would take a while, naturally, for news to spread of this simple human drama, which was also an historic event. Newman had been out of the limelight for a couple of years, in the quiet retirement of Littlemore. So many had been waiting to see what he would do, and often with an impending sense of dread. Now, as word began to go around that he had finally seceded from the Anglican Church, there were varying reactions. Soon there were large numbers of people, who had looked to him, following him into the Catholic Church. Much of public opinion in consequence became virulent in its denunciations of his defection, and he would end up becoming a social outcast in the eyes of many. Others, like Keble and Pusey, struggled to believe that what had happened was within God's providence. Pusey's words, in a public letter, were: 'He has gone as a simple act of duty with no view for himself, placing himself entirely in God's hands. And such are they whom God employs. He seems to me not so much gone from us, as transplanted into another part of the Vineyard, where the full energies of his powerful mind can be employed, which here they were not.'

Yet some of his closest friends had in fact already cut themselves off from him, and others would do so now. His own family felt shame, and only Jemima would try to remain a devoted sister, although unable to understand what he had done – and also in a difficult situation because of the anger her husband felt towards Newman. She reported too that their aunt, Elizabeth Newman, to whom Newman had always been devoted, had been very low at the prospect of his imminent conversion: 'She says it is the greatest grief that has ever befallen her, though she retracted it afterwards, and said we were always apt to look upon the present misfortune as the worst. I am very sorry to send you so painful a letter.'[12]

His own letter in reply to Jemima, like all he sent out at this time, expressed the strength of his conviction about his move, which was consistent 'with believing, as I firmly do, that individuals in the English Church are invisibly knit into that True Body of which they are not outwardly members'. He concluded: 'I will say nothing about my feelings all along to one so good and sweet as you are. There is One who knows how much it has lain upon my heart to pain you.' He enclosed a note to his aunt, who was able afterwards to speak of the 'sweet words' she received from her nephew.[13]

Later there was a moving letter to Keble, which would be his last for very many years. 'To you I owe it, humanly speaking, that I am what and where I am,' he wrote. Although others had helped in various ways, no one else but himself and Hurrell Froude had a part 'in setting my face in that special direction which has led me to my present inestimable gain'. Realising that his interpretation of Keble's help to him over the years might be difficult to accept, Newman concluded: 'Let this be your comfort, when you are troubled, to think that there is one who feels that he owes all to you, and who, though, alas, now cut off from you, is a faithful assiduous friend unseen.'[14]

And now, aged forty-four with less ability to adapt than would have been the case when he was younger, what was he facing into? Newman did not know. The Catholic Church, and its ways, and its people, was alien to him. He had prayed, and studied, and reflected until he knew he must enter into what he believed was 'the one Fold of the Redeemer'. What would that involve, humanly and personally? Only time would tell. But for the moment, there was certainly a great difference for the few Littlemore companions, as they slipped into Oxford as virtual strangers, 'to go to what to outward appearance is a meeting house', as Newman told Jemima, where twice a week they could attend Mass quietly.

In England Catholics were then a small peripheral group, gradually emerging from penal restrictions, some of them centred on the country houses of aristocrats and gentry, mainly in Lancashire and northern England, who had held onto much of their properties through dark centuries. These 'Old Catholics' had kept to themselves, and were ministered to by secretive priests. Latterly there was greater openness, and some migration into towns and cities as industrialisation progressed. For a time too there were thousands of émigrés, especially priests, refugees from the French Revolution, who had been welcomed into England. More permanent were growing numbers of religious and clerical establishments, including those also seeking safe refuge from the Terror in France. In addition, the poor Irish had been coming in since the beginning of the century, and just now were about to flood into the industrial areas, desperately driven from home as famine and death stalked Ireland. This was the world the Anglican and Oxford converts were entering into. It was incredibly at variance with what they had known, and inevitably there would be suspicion of them, and misunderstanding and conflict.

Step by step, Newman and his companions began entering into this different and new world. At the end of October they travelled up to see Nicolas Wiseman near Birmingham, now Coadjutor Bishop to the Vicar Apostolic of the Midland district, and also President at the impressive new Gothic, Pugin-designed Oscott College. It was the first meeting between Newman and Wiseman since the encounter in Rome in 1833, this time Newman finding himself initially crippled with shyness, and Wiseman at a loss for words too. Afterwards, on 1 November, the feast of All Saints, the little group was confirmed in Oscott's elaborate chapel. As for his incomplete book on development, which Newman handed over to him, Wiseman sensibly recommended that he publish it as it was. That is what he did, while simply adding at the end:

> Such were the thoughts concerning the 'Blessed Vision of Peace', of one whose long-continued petition had been that the Most Merciful would not despise the work of His own hands, nor leave him to himself; – while yet his eyes were dim, and his breast laden, and he could but employ Reason in the things of Faith. And now, dear Reader, time is short, eternity is long. Put not from you what you have here found; regard it not as a mere matter of present controversy; set not out resolved to refute it, and looking about for the best way of doing so; seduce not yourself with the imagination that it comes of disappointment, or disgust, or restlessness, or wounded feeling, or undue sensibility, or other weakness. Wrap not yourself round in the associations of years past; nor determine that to be truth which you wish to be so, nor make an idol of cherished anticipations. Time is short, eternity is long.[15]

With regard to the future, although Newman considered his Anglican ordination to be valid, he felt it might be better now to remain in Catholic lay life, because of his past record in opposing Roman Catholicism. But Wiseman persuaded him to seek ordination as a Catholic priest, and suggested that he and his group might be part of a body of priests engaged in apostolic work in the Midlands but with an intellectual emphasis. He mentioned in passing the example of the Oratorians, founded by St Philip Neri in sixteenth-century Rome, and this interested Newman. He also offered the group the use of Old Oscott, three miles away, sheltered in a valley, which had been the college until the large new establishment was built some years back. They went down to look at it, an old and rather forbidding place, and decided they would move there from Littlemore in the New Year, whenever it could be made ready. Newman later thought it should be called Maryvale – the name it has to this day.

Everything was so new, and so different. And yet from these beginnings of his Catholic life, something profound was fitting into place for Newman. For years he had studied and prayed and entered theologically into the Catholic dimension of Christian faith. He had fought for that dimension in the Church of his childhood, helped by others and influencing many in turn. The Anglican Church in most of its members and unanimously through its bishops had then rejected what he stood for. Pusey and Keble would continue steadfastly in it, and remain faithful to the Anglo-Catholicism they had espoused with him. Newman however had been condemned, and in any case his journey took him on further, out of a relative insularity, and into the wider Church centred on Rome. It was indeed a Church foreign to him in many respects. But in his innermost self there was a deep resonance with what he was finding. He had already a devotion to Mary, 'in whose College I lived, whose Altar I served'. Above all, his appreciation of the Eucharist was now indescribably fulfilled, as he realised the privilege of having the Blessed Sacrament near at hand, the sanctuary light in any Catholic chapel a sign of Christ's real presence there for the faithful. Again, he found himself easily adapting to Catholic devotion to the saints. And he valued too how Catholic teaching was authoritatively centred on the Holy See. In all this, in his mind and heart, he was at home.

Over the winter, Newman set out to visit many of the Catholic establishments across England, sometimes accompanied by Ambrose St John. 'We must throw ourselves into the system,' he said. Among places visited were the Trappist Monastery of Mount St Bernard in Leicestershire, the Bar Convent in York, Ushaw College near Durham, and Stonyhurst College in Lancashire. He also dealt personally with many who were following his example and heading Rome-wards, accompanying a nervous Maria Giberne for instance when she went for interview to Fr Brownbill, an eminent London Jesuit. Both Emily Bowles and Mary Holmes had already become Catholics, and would very often turn to him for advice. Many others, like William and Catherine Froude – especially Catherine – were continually discussing with him matters of faith, but unsure of where their searching would lead. His correspondence in any event was already huge, and would continue unabated for forty years. And, despite the deep but hidden pain of the loss of people dear to him, he was already starting to form some new friendships, including among them the Irishman Robert Whitty, whom he met at St Edmund's College in Ware – 'a more winning person I never saw', he reported to St John, 'I really seemed to form a sudden friendship with him.' Whitty, already a priest, would later try the Oratorian vocation, before eventually becoming a well-known Jesuit. The two of them would remain always on close terms.

February saw him back at Littlemore, sorting, burning, packing up, and engaged in the sad business of making last visits there. 'It is like going out on the open sea,' he wrote to St John, who was already at Old Oscott. He passed his forty-fifth birthday alone there, on 21 February 1846. The next day he left what had been his home for the past number of years – 'there it has been that I have both been taught my way and received an answer to my prayers', he wrote later to Copeland.[16] He walked to Mass in the Catholic Chapel, and then with Frederick Bowles stayed that night in Oxford, along with his friend, the astronomer Manuel Johnson, at the Radcliffe Observatory. They dined with a few including Copeland. Afterwards Richard Church called to say goodbye, and finally Pusey late into the night. Early the next morning, together with Bowles, he left for Birmingham. As he put it in the *Apologia*, eighteen years later:

> I left Oxford for good on Monday, February 23, 1846. On the Saturday and Sunday before, I was in my house at Littlemore simply by myself, as I had been for the first day or two when I had originally taken possession of it. I slept on Sunday night at my dear friend's, Mr Johnson's, at the Observatory. Various friends came to see the last of me … Dr Pusey too came to take leave of me; and I called on Dr Ogle, one of my very oldest friends, for he was my private Tutor, when I was an Undergraduate. In him I took leave of my first College, Trinity, which was so dear to me, and which held on its foundation so many who had been kind to me both when I was a boy, and all through my Oxford life. Trinity had never been unkind to me. There used to be much snap-dragon growing on the walls opposite my freshman's rooms there, and I had for years taken

it as the emblem of my own perpetual residence even unto death in my University. On the morning of 23 I left the Observatory. I have never seen Oxford since, excepting its spires, as they are seen from the railway.[17]

NOTES

1. *PS*, VIII, p. 242.
2. *LD*, IX, pp. 489–90.
3. Ibid., p. 515.
4. *Apo*, p. 147.
5. *SD*, p. 307.
6. *LD*, X, pp. 206–7.
7. Ibid., pp. 262–3.
8. *Dev*, p. 7.
9. Ibid., p. 40.
10. Ibid., p. 58.
11. Ibid., p. 90.
12. *LD*, XI, p. 13.
13. Ibid., p. 14.
14. Ibid., p. 34.
15. *Dev*, p. 443.
16. *LD*, XI, pp. 132–3.
17. *Apo*, pp. 236–7.

CHAPTER 5

Founding the Oratory

EWMAN NOW FOR a while was to come within the ambit and influence of Dr Nicolas Wiseman. He was one of four major Catholic churchmen in Britain and Ireland who would loom large in the rest of Newman's life. With three of these clerics, including Wiseman, his relations would come to grief. But this is not to take away from the positive and encouraging influence of Wiseman in the earlier years. Nicolas Wiseman had been born in Spain in 1802 into an Irish family originating from Waterford. After the early death of his father, his mother took him to live in Waterford for a while, before sending him to Ushaw College near Durham. Then his life was centred on the English College in Rome where, ordained a priest in 1825, he was distinguished in his studies, and had become its rector when Newman and Froude met him in 1833. In addition he became agent to the four bishops who were Vicars Apostolic in England. And now, making his own mark in the country, in a few years he would become England's first resident cardinal of the modern era.

At Oscott, he had already made good suggestions to Newman as to what he might do as a Catholic. But first Newman on his arrival at Maryvale, as he had now called it, just wanted to settle down with his companions and live within a Catholic atmosphere. The place itself had little to recommend it, with a high wall around and the windows barred. But the chapel with the Blessed Sacrament meant so much to him, confirming him in his decision to become a Catholic, as he thought now of the relative sense of emptiness in the churches he had known. When up in the bustling maelstrom of Oscott College he was often discomfited however, and having to conform to the many seminary observances. He even had to line up with the schoolboys for confession at Wiseman's door. Emily Bowles visited once, and found him in the Pugin chapel being made to answer catechism questions to an Italian priest. And sometimes he felt like a showpiece when visitors were there: 'I was the gaze of so many eyes at Oscott,' he wrote later, 'as if some wild incomprehensible beast, caught by the hunter, and a spectacle for Dr Wiseman to exhibit to strangers.'

In April he was told he would go to Rome to prepare for ordination. He had insisted on having a 'regular' Catholic education and now that he was to have it, the feeling was that of a boy being sent to a new school. The summer passed first, and it included his being with Elizabeth Bowden and her children in London when they were received into the Church. It was early September when he set out across the Channel with St John. They were feted by the French Church, and thought highly of the clergy they met. Later, five weeks were spent in Milan, Newman being fascinated by the place, especially the great Duomo, 'one of the most wonderful buildings in the world', with prayer and worship going on there incessantly. He loved Milan above all because it had been the see of Ambrose, and had associations with Monica, and of course Augustine, as well as with his beloved Athanasius, who had once come there when in exile.

Finally at the end of October they arrived in Rome itself. Their residence was the College of Propaganda, founded in the seventeenth century, along with the Roman Congregation of the same name – dedicated to the propagation of the faith in mission territories, and which included England under its jurisdiction. In the college, they found themselves among young men speaking more than thirty languages, all destined for missionary work across the world. Awkward in the black clerical clothes they had to wear, nevertheless they were put at their ease by the rector, Antonio Bresciani, 'a man of real delicacy as well as kindness', who was anxious to ease their lot, even to insisting they should have a tea-making machine installed in their quarters. St John, the better linguist, and more outgoing, was the one who had to do most of the talking with the Jesuit community there. Newman however was able to chat away to his confessor, Giuseppe Repetti, 'one of the holiest, most prudent men I ever knew', and he looked forward to his visits to Repetti's spartan room on cold evenings.

The rudimentary dogmatic and moral lectures they had to attend, until they were dispensed from them, often had Newman nodding and falling to sleep: '... anyhow you go, lecture after lecture, to drawl through a few tedious pages – All this is necessary for boys, not for grown men,' he wrote home.[1] And Newman's own theological outlook, especially as picked up in piecemeal translation from *The Development of Doctrine*, seemed to alarm the Roman authorities. He feared his book would be put on the Index, but eventually he was able to convince one of the best theologians, the Jesuit Giovanni Perrone, of his own orthodoxy, after he had boiled down his vision to a series of dry Latin propositions. In general, he was dismayed at the poor level of theology available – the Roman theologians, he felt, simply having no 'view'.

Although he liked the Jesuits very much, he reported to Jemima, in a free sharing of his views with her, that they were 'plodding, methodical, unromantic', and without the calculating shrewdness the world supposed them to have. He also remarked to her that they had a 'deep suspicion of change, with a perfect incapacity to create anything *positive* for the wants of the times'.[2] It was, after all, not long since the Jesuits had emerged from the trauma of their suppression by the Papacy – 'one of the most mysterious matters in the history of the Church', he thought – which resulted in their being particularly cautious at this time.

All along, keeping their special cloaks with them for the eventuality, they were expecting to be called to an audience with the Pope, the recently elected Pius IX. Suddenly the summons came, on a wet day in late November, and they dashed across to the Vatican, their cloaks collecting a deep brown mud as they went. After a long wait, they were ushered into the presence of the Pope. Awkward as he was on occasions such at this, Newman, when directed to kiss the

Papal foot, also managed to knock his head against the Papal knee. Otherwise the meeting went well, and Newman was able to report that the Pope was 'a vigorous man with a very pleasant countenance, and was most kind'. With a long and controversial reign ahead of him, the famous Pio Nono would often be displeased with what he heard of this Anglican convert, although on his side Newman would retain a warm personal regard for the Pope.

Indeed, he soon incurred the Pope's mild censure, when he was pressed into preaching at the funeral of a niece of Lady Shrewsbury, much against his better judgment. It was really a gossiping society occasion, with Catholics bringing their Protestant friends, and Newman 'saying nothing right', as he put it later, 'not from want of tact so much as from sheer ignorance'. Undiplomatically, he stressed the need for a change of heart in this life, to prepare for the next, which did not go down well. The Pope, hearing about it, remarked that honey was more suitable than vinegar on such occasions, while one of the Protestant visitors suggested – it was reported to Newman – that he ought to be 'thrown into the Tyber'.

Over the winter, the question of what he and his companions should do became clear to Newman. A visit to the Roman Oratory made a great impression on him, and he thought again of Wiseman's suggestion that they might become Oratorians. Founded by St Philip Neri in sixteenth-century Rome, they were not a religious order but groups of secular priests living together, and under a simple Rule. Each house of the Oratory, which was independent, had a church attached, and was situated in a town. It offered opportunities for learning and scholarship, while also being involved in active pastoral work. The individual members, retaining their private means of income, could have their own particular sphere of activity. They were without vows – and therefore, as an 'unarmed weaponless state',[3] as he said later, had a special requirement to learn in friendship to cooperate together, as a true community. Newman was struck by all of this. Helped by the guidance of Fr Repetti, he saw that joining a religious order was out of the question, whereas the Oratory would ensure a continuity especially with what he and his companions had lived in such as Oxford colleges – although he did not intend his future companions to come exclusively from that background. Moreover, he was much drawn to the spirit of St Philip Neri himself, known as 'the Apostle of Rome'. He thought St Philip was very like Keble, in his humour yet serious intent, hatred of humbug and tender love of others.

With prayer, and careful study of the history and spirit of the Oratorians, Newman and St John became convinced their vocation was to be with them. The Pope himself was delighted with the idea, allowing Newman to revise the Rule to suit conditions in England – which he did with great thought and effort. Newman could see possibilities for Oratories in the modern expanding centres of population in Britain, starting out from Birmingham, each with its own characteristics and accommodated to members with different interests and talents. He was aware of his own age now, having less energy than before, and feeling himself 'so stiff and wooden'. The Oratory would suit him, while allowing scope to the younger people, with whom he might be a 'bond of union'. And the sense of continuity was important to him. If he had joined a religious order, he would have to start all over again. In any case, the orders as he saw them tended to crush the freedom and spontaneity of the individual member. If he were a Jesuit, for instance, 'no one would know that I was speaking my own words'.[4] But in the Oratory, the work he had begun at Oxford might be continued in some way, if God so willed it, allowing him to remain himself and to speak with his own voice.

After Easter, Newman made a nine-day retreat with the Jesuits for his ordination. During it he made notes for himself in Latin, in which he reproached himself for his love of ease, his timidity and lack of a lively faith. His prayer was very poor, more a crawling along the ground than exhibiting any ability to fly, as he put it, and the meditations he was expected to do making his head tired. He felt his best years were behind him, and considered that he would make a poor Oratorian.[5] Yet, released from the retreat, he was in good spirits and enjoyed some trips in the spring weather to beautiful and historical places around Rome. Meanwhile, as the Pope had stipulated that the various companions should make a short novitiate in common, they were gathering in from England and France: Dalgairns, Stanton, Bowles, William Penny and Robert Coffin.

However Neman had a scruple before his ordination. Although later he became unsure about the validity of his Anglican orders, at this time he looked on them as valid, and mentioned this to Cardinal Fransoni, who was to be the ordaining prelate. Fransoni in reply said he believed Newman and his companions were priests already, and so they should understand that their Catholic ordination would be conditional. This put Newman's mind at rest. Ordained a deacon with Ambrose St John on 29 May 1847, the two of them were ordained Catholic priests in the chapel of Propaganda the next morning. Newman said his first Mass some days later, on the feast of Corpus Christi, and on the following day he said the Jesuit community Mass at Propaganda.

Soon it was time to leave that college, where they had been so happy. Newman however left a memorandum with the rector, outlining what he had picked up of discontent among the English-speaking students, and suggesting ways which might make for improved training and personal formation, including outside contacts, better reading, and opportunities for theological and philosophical discussion, all of which would be more suited to maturing adults, and prepare them more realistically to deal with the world they would encounter. Then he was off with the other members of his Maryvale group to make their Oratorian novitiate, in the surroundings of the beautiful Cistercian monastery at Santa Croce. In contrast to Propaganda, his novitiate under Fr Carlo Rossi of the Roman Oratory was 'dreary', with 'room-sweeping, slop-emptying, dinner-serving, bed making, shoe blacking'. Fr Rossi himself was apparently opinionated and excitable, and Newman ill at ease with him. But at least their regime allowed for some more trips for the group, especially when they went to Naples and experienced the kindness and hospitality of the Oratory there.

At the end of November the Papal Brief arrived, making Newman Superior for life of the English Oratory, and authorising him to set up the first house in Birmingham. Fr Rossi relinquished his English convert charges, and soon Newman and St John were on their way home, hurrying to escape the closure of the Alps by snow. They went via Munich, to visit the great German Catholic Church historian Dr Ignaz Döllinger, who had first made contact with Newman after the publication of his *Lectures on Justification*. Then they rushed by train to Ostend, crossed the Channel in fog and snow, and arrived back in England on Christmas Eve. He said his first Mass on home soil in Elizabeth Bowden's private chapel in London on Christmas Day, with his godson Charlie Bowden serving.

At Christmas lunch with Wiseman, who had now moved from the Midlands to be pro-Vicar Apostolic of the London District, Newman learned that another group under Frederick William Faber wished to join the Oratory. Thirteen years younger than Newman, Faber had been very influenced by him at Oxford, and had gone over to Rome only a few weeks after Newman's conversion, and then founded his own community called 'Brothers of the Will of God', or 'Wilfridians', all of them converts from his former Anglican parish, many of them very young. They had established themselves in a country area, at Cheadle in Staffordshire, which they called St Wilfrid's, and which was near Alton Towers, the seat of Lord Shrewsbury. At one time a budding poet, Faber was given to colourful emotional extremes, and already had been virulent in his attacks on members of his former Church, much to the distaste of Newman. As for his community, the insightful Fr Dominic Barberi had humorously rechristened them 'Brothers of the Will of Faber'. His decision to attach himself and his followers to Newman's Oratorians, and to 'surrender' himself to Newman, came as a sudden 'inspiration', and was of a piece with his own devotionalism. Newman was reluctant to accept them, but Wiseman was in favour, as were his own companions, and in the end he agreed to the merger.

On 2 February 1848, Feast of the Purification (also Oriel's foundation day), the English Congregation of the Oratory was set up by Newman in Maryvale. Ten days later he travelled up to Cheadle to receive the community there, seventeen in all, with just two of them priests, Faber and Anthony Hutchison. Newman immediately found himself saddled, not only with the new large and volatile youthful group, but also with the headache of what to do with the distant country property of St Wilfrid's. Faber, despite protestations of complete obedience to Newman, required an immediate resolution, preferably that of giving up Maryvale and everyone heading away up to Staffordshire. But Newman at this stage felt St Wifrid's was a burden, and wanted to be rid of it, much to the annoyance of Lord Shrewsbury, who had given financial help to it on condition that the church was served by a religious community.

At the same time he was preaching on eight successive Sundays in St Chad's Cathedral. On these occasions, he nearly always walked in and out the six miles to Pugin's red-brick gothic edifice, with its twin spires, recently erected in the middle of Birmingham. His offerings were good but ordinary enough, perhaps as a result of his feeling his way. Yet his voice and simple bearing were striking. After the second sermon, he gave up reading his text, as was the Anglican custom, and instead preached directly to the congregation. Helping the priests at St Chad's at this time indeed became the very first work of the Oratorians. And he also published anonymously a novel entitled *Loss and Gain: The Story of a Convert*, detailing in an often amusing way the story of one Charles Reding who journeys from Anglicanism to Rome. It had been written during spare time in Rome, partly as an effort to help 'poor Burns' – James Burns, the convert founder of the publishing firm Burns and Oates. He only put his name expressly to the book in 1874, although many knew the author's identity from the beginning. Publishing a novel seemed such a 'come-down' for the former eminent Anglican divine, with some earnest souls expressing the view, as Faber told him, that he had 'sunk below Dickens'.

Faber's group eventually had to make some kind of a novitiate, and unfortunately Newman put Faber himself in charge of it, who really could not take the necessary responsibility, resulting in matters becoming sometimes chaotic. Next, Newman gave up Maryvale, and went to the great trouble of moving with all of the community to St Wilfrid's for the time being, it proving impossible to keep up the two places. But he was also looking to the long term, arranging for a suitable site in Birmingham itself. This was the wish of the new Vicar Apostolic in the Midlands, Bishop William Ullathorne, in addition to it being specified in the Papal Brief. He was also actively investigating where a second Oratory could be established in London, partly because many of them wanted to go there, Faber especially having it in his sights now, rather than St Wilfrid's, in order to be at the centre of things.

The successor to Wiseman in the Midlands was to have lasting and positive significance for Newman and the Oratorians who would remain in Birmingham. William Bernard Ullathorne, now Vicar Apostolic and soon to be Bishop of Birmingham, came from an old Catholic family in Yorkshire, and was a descendant of St Thomas More. Born in 1806, he had been a cabin boy at sea initially, and then joined the Benedictines at Downside. As a priest, he had spent ten years in Australia, his revelations of the dreadful transportation system helping to bring about its abolition. Then stationed in Coventry, he next became Vicar Apostolic of the Western District before coming to replace Wiseman. A devout, shrewd and forthright man, imbued with the Benedictine spirit, he was to make an outstanding contribution to the building up of Catholic life in the large Midland area over which he had responsibility.

As Newman was grappling with all the problems, especially the human ones, surrounding him at this stage, he was also having his first dealings with Ullathorne. Not all augured well at the beginning. Faber had been producing translations of a continental series of saints' lives, of a florid and extravagant nature, which were not calculated to appeal to the sensible and restrained Old Catholics. Ullathorne wanted their publication ended, but Newman, despite his own personal dislike of such hagiography, wanted to support Faber. Ullathorne had good reason to be wary of some of the converts, such as Faber with his Romanising tendencies, and the architect Pugin with his fanatical promotion of Gothic churches and rood screens. But he tended at first to categorise Newman and the Oratorians in general among them, although he was still keen to have their services. Newman on his part, leaning backwards to accommodate Faber and the younger men, and really for a while under their sway, tended to be reserved initially in his dealings with Ullathorne. Soon however each was becoming more aware of the worth of the other – and 'out of the little rubs we have had', as Ullathorne put it, and despite differences of opinion, a deep mutual regard was forged, which would last for the next forty years.

The person who really brought them together, Newman believed, was the extraordinary Mother Margaret Hallahan, founder of her own congregation of Dominican nuns. A year younger than Newman, Margaret had been born in extreme poverty, in London's East End, to Irish parents. An only child, she lost both her father and mother when aged nine, and found herself in an orphanage. After many difficult situations working as a family servant, including in Belgium, she became a Dominican Tertiary, and Ullathorne's housekeeper in Coventry. She then began to gather around herself a group of women devoted to prayer and to the poor, who were constituted as Dominicans under the patronage of St Catherine of Siena. Margaret would also become Ullathorne's closest lifelong friend. And when she met Newman first, before he went to Rome, she had great feeling for him – and, despite their so different backgrounds, they found an immediate mutual understanding. It was this that made the difference, as she now conveyed to Ullathorne all she felt about Newman. Intuitively, she wrote once: 'I am so sorry for Dr Newman, it seems as if he could not do right, do what he will. It will all be known when he is dead.'

Towards the end of 1848 a place became available in Birmingham, on Alcester Street, towards Deritend, where the Oratorians could, at least in the shorter term, set up a much-needed mission. The building, despite having a classical-style façade, had been a gin distillery, and Newman felt it would suit their purposes, especially as it had a long room which could be converted into a chapel. The lease was bought, and its adaptation started at once. In late January Newman moved in, the chapel was opened on 2 February, again the Feast of the Purification, and soon the group found themselves hard at work. They were in the thickly populated outskirts of the growing city, in a district full of small factories, warehouses and rows of little brick houses. Parts of the canal system ran through the area, and nearby too was the expanding railway network, including the already busy London & North Western route via Coventry and Rugby to the capital. All around were all the poor and often migrant families, out of which came the pools of unskilled labour for the press-factories turning out the cheap wares for which Birmingham was known.

At that time there were only small numbers of Catholics in Birmingham, whose inhabitants tended to be Nonconformist insofar as they were religious at all. But there were very poor Irish arriving, these being the years of the Great Irish Famine, and the Oratorians wished to minister especially to these. They started up talks in the evenings, to try to attract people after work, and were surprised at how many children turned up. 'Boys and girls flow in for instruction as herrings in season', Newman wrote, referring to the poor young factory workers who started coming their way, many of them unbaptised. Indeed, initial thoughts of opening a school had to be abandoned, once they realised that most of the children aged over seven were in fact working all day until late in the evening. So it was that much of the Oratory's weekday work was crowded into the hours between seven o'clock and nine o'clock in the evening.

On Sundays their makeshift chapel was full and sometimes overflowing, both at the morning Masses and at evening Benediction, Newman occasionally having the job of organist. His own sermons at this time had quite an effect in Birmingham, with crowds turning up to hear him, Protestant and Catholic alike. Published at the end of 1849 as *Discourses to Mixed Congregations*, they are somewhat in the line of Catholic missionary preaching then, often with a strong emphasis on the eternal consequences of how we live here, and perhaps without a sufficient portrayal of the great attractiveness of the Gospel. Ornate in language, they lack the great enduring simplicity of his Oxford parochial days – although some have their own severe beauty, such as 'Mysteries of Nature and Grace', and 'The Mystery of Divine Condescension'. But once again his hearers were struck by his bearing, by his simple unworldliness and evident care and concern. What really mattered for him, of course, and for his Catholic congregation, was the consoling and uplifting experience of the Mass itself, whether simply said, or sung with the music of Plainchant. And for the Irish people present, the familiarity of the church setting, and the kindliness of the fathers, meant so much, helping to stabilise their lives and give them a sense of meaning and worth.

In September 1849 Newman was ill with one of the heavy colds to which he was prone when overworked. Just then there was an outbreak of the dreaded cholera at Bilston, outside Wolverhampton, and at Ullathorne's request, he set out to help, along with Ambrose St John, and Br Aloysius Boland, one of the young laybrothers they had at that time. Their departure set everyone in Deritend 'crying out as if we were going to be killed', he wrote, noting how the parish had created 'a *local mass* of affection' for his community. But the people need not have worried. As matters turned out, the cholera was abating at Bilston when they arrived there, and there was little they were required to do.

Their own internal Oratorian problems had continued, however, and it took a while to arrange a separate Oratory in London, where Newman agreed Faber could go, and also those who might like to be around him and out of the back streets of Birmingham. At first they got a premises on King William Street, off the Strand, in central London, and Faber moved down there at the end of April. Elizabeth Bowden helped him set up the place, and her son John moved in as a novice, with Charlie following later. With frenetic energy Faber had the London Oratory open in June, Newman sending him most of the best people to form the community, and to ensure the success of the venture. They got going in style, Newman brought down to preach, but relieved to head back afterwards to his more modest surroundings. Soon the London Oratorians were becoming influential in London circles, including in high society, and were making important converts.

In 1850 Newman was again down in London, at the behest of Wiseman, to deliver a series of lectures at the Oratory. He had been uncertain what to speak about, but in March what was called the Gorham Judgment gave him a direction, when in effect the government overruled the Anglican Bishop of Exeter, who had refused to institute Rev G.C. Gorham to a living because his views on baptismal regeneration were unsound. The ruling was to lead to a new wave of Anglicans entering the Catholic Church, including Newman's friends James Hope and Robert Wilberforce, as well as Henry Edward Manning, who had been Archdeacon of Chichester.

Beginning in early May, and continuing generally at the rate of two a week until into July, Newman gave his London talks which were then published as *Lectures on Certain Difficulties felt by Anglicans in submitting to the Catholic Church*. They outlined what he believed were the intrinsic contradictions in Anglicanism, whose Protestantism would not allow for the Catholic dimension, so that the Tractarians really had no convincing alternative but to enter the Catholic Church itself. Humour and satire were employed by him, and, although he wished to avoid giving offence to seriously enquiring former co-religionists, he was quite devastating and polemical in his views.

Wiseman himself attended the Oratory lectures, as well as various well-known people, including William Makepeace Thackeray. Henry Wilberforce came once, and his wife Mary became a Catholic in June, while he himself later in the autumn was received in Brussels. In time Henry's Tractarian theologian brother Robert came over as well, and their eldest brother William – leaving only their brother Sam as an Anglican (who became Bishop of Oxford). As a result of these lectures and their influence, Newman was awarded an honourary pontifical doctorate of divinity. Often called 'Mr Newman' up to now, especially by Ullathorne, he was henceforth officially referred to as 'Dr Newman'.

In October the London Oratory was set up as an autonomous house, Faber being elected its first superior, but Newman agreeing to be in a consultative capacity to them for three years. At this stage he finally persuaded the Londoners to take charge of St Wilfrid's. He had hoped for a while that it might become a joint holiday house for the two communities, but now it was clear that its disposal was necessary. Robert Coffin had remained out there as its rector. Newman initially had wanted Coffin to take charge in London, but such was Faber's hostility to him that he had relented on his choice. Around the time of the disposal of St Wilfrid's, Coffin left the congregation, disillusioned with it, and subsequently became a Redemptorist, rising to be Provincial, and later Bishop of Southwark. His was not the only significant loss to the Oratory. The excellent Robert Whitty, whom Newman had met at St Edmund's College in Ware, and who a good while past had promised to join them, had finally arrived at Christmas 1848. Now he left too, and his departure was felt keenly. Faber had also shown antipathy towards him, because he was Irish – and displayed a similar attitude to another talented Irishman now in the Birmingham Oratory, John Stanislas Flanagan. Newman would remain on good terms with Whitty, who first became Vicar General to Wiseman in London, then joined the Jesuits, becoming Provincial in England, and Assistant to the Jesuit General in Rome. The loss of these individuals, and of others in the coming years, would be a huge blow to Newman's hopes for the Oratory in England.

But wider important events overshadowed the separation of the two Oratories. At the end of September a Papal Brief was issued restoring the Catholic hierarchy in England and Wales, with Wiseman made Cardinal Archbishop of Westminster in London, and Ullathorne Bishop of the new Birmingham diocese. Like some others, Newman had doubted the wisdom of the move, and in any case wished it were done quietly. But Wiseman, from the safe confines of Rome, rashly sent ahead a flamboyant pastoral, 'From out the Flaminian Gate', which was preached from all pulpits on 20 October. 'Catholic England has been restored to its orbit in the ecclesiastical firmament', the pastoral boasted. The result was a public outcry. Despite the religious and political advances in the past decades, there was still an elemental English fear of Roman domination, which now was vented in 'No Popery' riots and the vilification of Catholics. The Puseyites, as the Catholic-minded Anglicans were generally known now, were subjected to particular hostility, as traitors within the camp. Even the liberal Whig Prime Minister, Lord John Russell, joined the hue and cry against the 'Papal Aggression', and brought in the Ecclesiastical Titles Act, directed against anyone assuming a title to a 'pretended' see.

When Cardinal Wiseman arrived back in London, however, he brought out his *Appeal to the English People*, a pamphlet that was widely distributed, and printed in full in the main newspapers. In it he highlighted the growth in England of religious toleration – and, in response to the affronted Chapter of Westminster Abbey, who thought his title implied jurisdiction over them, he said he would not encroach upon their ministry to the fashionable and wealthy, but instead would claim the many poor of the City of Westminster as his own. A brilliant piece of work, the pamphlet succeeded in its purpose, in helping more thoughtful people to abandon their hostility. Soon the Cardinal followed up with a series of striking lectures in the new Southwark Cathedral, which again had an effect. Newman was lost in admiration for Wiseman's achievement. 'He is made for the world,' he wrote to a friend, 'and he rises with the occasion. Highly as I put his gifts I was not prepared for such a display of vigour, power, and judgment as the last two months have brought. I heard a dear friend of his say before he had got to England that the news of the opposition would kill him. How he has been out. It is the event of the time. In my own remembrance there has been nothing like it.'[6]

The Birmingham Catholics had their own share of discomfiture, and Newman himself was also a national figure of hate, the satirical magazine *Punch* becoming very anti-Catholic, publishing vicious caricatures of him and Wiseman. On 27 October 1850, at the installation of Ullathorne as Bishop of Birmingham in St Chad's, Newman gave a long sermon entitled 'Christ upon the Waters', addressing the present situation with his own satire and historical insight, while calling for robust and steady faith in the providential workings of God.[7] He was well used to controversy and conflict, and was now drawing upon his experience to encourage others to be bold and not governed by fear. Between June and September 1851 he entered the fray himself more publicly, delivering a series of lectures in the Birmingham Corn Exchange, which would be published as *Lectures on the Present Position of Catholics in England*. He was in fighting form when he gave them, confronting the anti-Catholicism of the Established Church, and the still deep-seated prejudices of Protestantism. With humour and remorseless sarcasm he set out to puncture the insularity and complacency of 'John Bull', while yet, as an Englishman himself, honouring the English love for justice and fairness, but which had been conspicuously absent where Catholicism was concerned.

In late July 1851, in the fifth of his lectures, Newman made a personal indictment against an Italian ex-Dominican priest named

Achilli, who had been employed by the Protestant Evangelical Alliance to denounce the corruptions of Rome. Previously, Wiseman in the *Dublin Review* had outlined how Achilli had been found guilty by the Roman Inquisition of sexual immorality and assault, and imprisoned. Little notice had been taken of Wiseman's article, and so Newman, after taking advice from a few legal friends, decided to repeat its charges in one of his lectures, where they could not be ignored. It was a calculated risk, and, although it succeeded in stopping the Evangelical Alliance's campaign, Newman soon found that Achilli was determined to take legal action against him for libel. Unfortunately, Wiseman then failed to produce the papers on which his allegations were based, and Nicholas Darnell and Joseph Gordon from the Birmingham Oratory had to set out to Italy to collect fresh documents and evidence. Newman's lawyers advised him not to fight the case because of the prevailing anti-Catholic prejudice. But even though he found in November that he would have to stand trial, and on a criminal charge, with the prospect of imprisonment if found guilty, Newman felt he could not withdraw, as to do so would betray the Catholic cause. The time ahead would be a stressful one, exacerbated above all by the uncertain waiting.

Throughout the weeks and months of these years, the ordinary hidden work went on at Alcester Street, 'amid our labyrinth of lanes and beneath our firmament of smoke', with Newman taking his share of preaching, instructing and confessing. A significant addition to the community was the gentle Edward Caswall, a widower and former Anglican clergyman. A poet, his translations of the hymns of the Breviary were noteworthy, as for instance the beautiful Advent hymn, 'Hear the herald voice resounding', which is still in use. He brought a considerable endowment to the Oratory, and in consequence it was decided to build a more permanent community house, with church attached. The site chosen was that of the present Oratory, on the Hagley Road in Edgbaston, then on the western edge of Birmingham. The professional classes and business people were coming to reside here, while also, from the pastoral point of view, there would be increasing numbers of less well-off people to be catered for as well, especially in the neighbouring areas of Ladywood and Smethwick.

The new large Edgbaston house was designed by the Irish railway engineer Terence Flanagan, brother of Stanislas. As for the church, there were no funds available then to build an elaborate one, so work had to go ahead on a very basic structure, which would be fitted with a second-hand roof acquired from a disused factory. Nevertheless, much care would be taken in adorning it. For want of a better term, Newman would describe it as being in a 'Roman style'. Work progressed well on the house, and during Lent 1852 the community were on the move to their new home. The church would not be ready for more than another eighteen months. Across town, Alcester Street would still be served by them for some years, until it became a regular parish in the diocese. Going out to Edgbaston was to be the last of those wearisome major house moves Newman made, although just now and in the next number of years he was to have a domicile of sorts over in Dublin, crossing the Irish Sea again and again, in the quest to help Archbishop Cullen there set up the Catholic University.

NOTES

1. *LD*, XII, p. 48.
2. Ibid., pp. 25–6, 103–4.
3. Dom Placid Murray, *Newman the Oratorian*, Dublin: Gill and Macmillan, 1969, p. 375.
4. *LD*, XI, p. 306.
5. cf. *AW*, pp. 245–8.
6. *LD*, XIV, p. 185.
7. *SVO*, pp. 121–62.

— CHAPTER 6 —

The University
in Dublin

IT WAS BACK in April 1851 when Newman received a letter from Paul Cullen, the new Archbishop of Armagh, looking for suggestions about a proposed Catholic University in Ireland, and in addition asking him to come over to give some lectures on education. In Ireland, the question of university education for Catholics had been a vexed one, which Sir Robert Peel had addressed in 1845 by moving a bill to set up the secular and non-denominational Queen's Colleges, and which would provide an alternative to the Anglican Trinity College in Dublin. Some of the Irish Catholic bishops, including Archbishop Daniel Murray in Dublin, were in favour, while others were against the government's plan. Rome itself spoke of 'the grave danger to the Catholic faith' represented by the measure, and urged the setting up of a Catholic University after the example of Louvain, which the Belgian bishops had recently re-established. Archbishop Murray however, with the wisdom of long experience in gaining concessions for his people, still saw room for manoeuvre with London, which could lead to a good deal for Catholics. But significantly Cullen, first as Rector of the Irish College in Rome, and then when appointed Archbishop of Armagh in 1850, and in addition given the powers of Apostolic Delegate, was totally against the notion of mixed higher education. He and the other opponents would simply refer to what the government was setting up as 'Godless colleges', over which there could be no negotiation.

Newman for his part had been very concerned about the lack of good education among the laity, and indeed the clergy, in the Church. He was conscious that with his own intellectual background he could be of help in this regard – but how, he did not know. He also felt deeply for the married converts, most of whom had been in Anglican orders, in some cases now impoverished, and generally as lay people without any role in the service of the Church they had joined. Here were highly educated men, their heroism in becoming and remaining Catholics hardly recognised, and their talents unused. Such people could be of immense benefit to Catholicism, he believed, and their services would surely be needed in the times ahead.

And now there came this idea of a Catholic University. Newman was enthused by what he heard from Cullen, as he had himself for years wished the Church had such an institution. In agreement with Cullen, he considered the University might serve not just Ireland but the wider English-speaking world. It could therefore be a transposition of what he had fought for at Oxford, in championing a worthy religious ethos against the prevailing secularising currents. He thought too of how some of the very able convert laymen could be brought into such a venture. A few months later, in July 1851 – the month when the fateful references were made to Achilli in one of the Corn Market lectures – Cullen came himself to see Newman in Birmingham, offering him the rectorship of the University, to which Newman eventually agreed. But he did not wish to be in breach of his first duties at the Oratory, and so expressed the hope that his duties would entail 'as little absence as possible' from his community. He was next appointed by Cullen on a subcommittee making plans for the University, agreed to give lectures in Dublin, and in October travelled for the first time to Ireland, and down from Dublin to Thurles to help give the report of the subcommittee's work, which drew especially on what they had learned about Louvain. In November – when he also found he was to be sent for trial – the Catholic University Committee, headed by Cullen, appointed him as Rector.

Another three years were to pass by, however, before the University itself would be constituted, which was frustrating, as he intended giving only a limited period of time to the venture. Cullen had advised caution, in view of Archbishop Murray's lack of support. In any case Newman had a lot to occupy him at home in the early months of 1852. There were community matters and the parish to be dealt with, as well as all the work around the move to Edgbaston. A crisis erupted in the London Oratory, with Faber becoming ill, and others there, rebelling against his erratic rule, appealing to Newman to sort things out. There was for him the real worry of the impending trial, dealings with lawyers, and the search for evidence and witnesses in Italy, with Maria Giberne also involved in contacting and looking after women who could be persuaded to come and testify against Achilli in England. The 'Newman Defence Fund' was set up in London, comprising some wealthy and influential friends of his, including the convert Irish MP William Monsell. Especially consoling were the subscriptions coming in from Ireland, Cullen being active in this regard.

Newman himself was asking for prayers, above all from Margaret Hallahan and her Dominican sisters. Mother Margaret urged him to have recourse to Mary Refuge of Sinners: 'She will be sure to gain the victory for you.' Newman wrote to Sister Imelda Poole, another friend of his in the community, 'I have this difficulty, that it is taxing our Blessed Lady unfairly' to expect her intervention to get him acquitted in such unlikely circumstances. His caution led Margaret herself to scold him about his lack of faith in the Mother of God, to which he replied: 'Thank you with all my heart for what you are so kindly intending to gain for me. Thank you also for the reproof you have administered to me. I know well I am an unbelieving old beast; and so perhaps in this instance.'

Over much of this year, and in the midst of all these other concerns, Newman worked away, both at the lectures he was expected to give, where he kept in mind suggestions offered by Archbishop Cullen, and at the subsequent discourses which would not be delivered but only published, but which were necessary to round off his understanding of university education. He sought advice on them from a number of sources, above all from Dr David Moriarty, President of All Hallows Missionary College, with whom he became especially friendly.

Another advisor, but more on how generally he should approach matters in Ireland, was Frederick Lucas, founder and editor of the Catholic weekly *The Tablet*. An English convert from Quakerism, Lucas had moved publication of *The Tablet* over to Dublin in 1849, and was championing Irish rights, becoming a friend of the 'Lion of the West', the great nationalistic Archbishop John MacHale of Tuam – and as a consequence incurring the enmity of the Roman-minded Cullen, who as Apostolic Delegate was working to curb the independence and stop the political agitation of MacHale and those around him. Unfortunately for the University, Newman in time would be caught unwittingly in the middle of this irreconcilable rift in the Irish Church, despite wishing to serve Cullen and at the same time be true to his regard for Lucas.

Prospects for starting the University seemed to improve when Daniel Murray died at the end of February, after a sudden illness, with Cullen then being appointed to succeed him as Archbishop of Dublin in the springtime. For two weeks in May Newman had lodgings at 22 Lower Dorset Street, taking advantage of the location to walk around each morning to the Jesuits in Gardiner Street, to say Mass, and have breakfast. He then rented out a room in the fashionable school of a Dublin priest, Dr James Quinn (later Bishop of Brisbane) at 16–17 Harcourt Street, where he could stay whenever he was in Dublin, and in which he could leave his papers and other belongings in between visits. His weekly lectures, five in all, took place in the assembly rooms at the Rotunda, starting on Monday 10 May, with a quick visit to Birmingham between the third and fourth lectures, and the final one given on Monday 7 June. He was gratified and encouraged by the numbers who came to hear him, the room where he gave his first lecture almost filled to its capacity of four hundred, 'all the intellect, almost of Dublin' he heard being there, including thirteen Trinity fellows, eight Jesuits, and a great many clergy. Although he had sought much advice in their composition, he had been very anxious before their delivery, but now felt they had gone off far better than he could have expected.

Straightaway after his last discourse he headed back to England. His trial in London had been delayed by stratagems of the prosecution lawyers, and untruths they put out, once they realised that good witnesses had arrived from Italy – all of which Newman detailed in a letter to Sister Imelda Poole, and which led him to conclude: 'Yet Achilli's solicitors *who do all this* are highly respectable men. Is it not wonderful?' Now the trial was going ahead, and it began on 21 June, and lasted in all five days. Newman was stopped by his lawyers from attending in person, so that he spent most of the time before the Blessed Sacrament in the King William Street chapel. The prejudice of the court, judge and jury, was palpable. In addition he felt that his own principal counsel, the Attorney General, Sir Alexander Cockburn, was not really on his side, and considered him at one point guilty of 'treachery'. So despite the combined and dignified evidence of the women who had been brought from Italy, it came as no surprise when the verdict went against him.

He refused to be downcast, but now had to wait for the sentence, which was postponed until November. He wrote to Margaret Hallahan thanking her and the community for their prayers: 'In gaining so many prayers, I gain an inestimable benefit. Whoever loses, I gain … Mary is taking the best way, depend on it, for our victory.' And certainly there were thoughtful observers who saw the injustice of the court. In a leading article, condemning the trial's proceedings and verdict, the *Times* newspaper said that 'a great blow has been given to the administration of justice in this country, and that Roman Catholics will henceforth have only too good reason for asserting that there is no justice for them in cases tending to arouse the Protestant feelings of judges and juries'.

Immediately he crossed over to Dublin again, for Cullen's installation as Archbishop. Next he was back in Birmingham, and went up to Oscott to deliver his famous sermon, 'The Second Spring', at the first synod of the new hierarchy. His preaching there to the assembled prelates and heads of religious orders was an extraordinary evocation of the hopes held out then for the restoration of Catholicism in England, poignantly remembering the tribulations of the past centuries, and looking to a new springtime, where a resurgent Church 'ever young' would rival the former glories which were lost.[1] Then came for him the upsetting news that his estranged sister

Harriet had died. Soon he had word too of the death of his aunt Elizabeth, whom he loved, and who had been very good to him as a child. Pierced with pain at her distress when he became a Catholic, he later had little contact with her, as she lived with the Mozleys in Derby, where he had not been invited for some years now.

He was seriously worn out by all that had happened. Back he went to Ireland for a fortnight, travelling to gain support for the University. He managed to spend a week alone, resting in the house and grounds of William Monsell at Tervoe, by the River Shannon a few miles downstream from Limerick. Gradually he completed the rest of his discourses, having them published individually in Dublin by James Duffy, the final one printed at the end of November. In London that month an application was made for a retrial, which was argued in January, but refused, quite clearly because of the prospect of humiliation for the trial judge, Lord Campbell, who was the Chief Justice. Meanwhile, still run down, Newman was made to get further rest, going up to Scotland to stay at Abbotsford, once the home of Sir Walter Scott, and now that of his great lawyer-friend James Hope, who had taken the name of Hope-Scott on marrying Scott's granddaughter and heir.

From there he was called back to court in London on 31 January to hear his fate – which turned out to be only a one hundred pound fine, or imprisonment until it was paid. The sentencing judge, Sir John Coleridge, formerly a Tractarian admirer, in a speech which Newman noted was full of mistakes and inconsistencies, said his charges against Achilli were probably exaggerated, and put it down to his deterioration since becoming a Catholic. The paltry fine itself was the equivalent of an acquittal – and Newman, who had brought some personal belongings expecting to go straight to prison, instead walked out of the court with his friends, once the fine was paid, to be cheered by a group of supporters who had gathered outside. That evening he wrote to Sister Imelda Poole: 'Thank you for all I have gained from your prayers. Every kind thought of Reverend Mother and your whole community.' And at least it was the end of Achilli, and the Evangelical Alliance's use of him, as he disappeared from view, and soon afterwards left the country.

Soon there was more personal loss, with the death of Joseph Gordon, who with Henry Austin Mills and Nicholas Darnell was a member of Faber's group remaining on in Birmingham. Ill for a time, the outstanding Fr Gordon had been regarded by Newman as 'the *life* of our Oratory', and a solid support in all the past troubles. Earlier, too, Br Aloysius Boland, who had accompanied Newman in helping the Bilston cholera victims, had been taken from them. Born in Ireland, in Westmeath, and christened Robert, he came to Birmingham at the age of nineteen in 1844, and joined Faber's Wilfridians. Admitted among the original group of Oratorians constituted on 2 February 1848 at Maryvale, Aloysius was one of the laybrothers they had for a number of these years. He died of consumption on 19 March 1852, which was St Joseph's Day.

It is astonishing to realise that Newman, in between all the events crowding the year of 1852 for him, still managed to turn out such a classic as his university discourses. Gathered together in one volume, they were published in February 1853 as *Discourses on the Scope and Nature of University Education: Addressed to the Catholics of Dublin.* Their composition had caused him more trouble than anything else he had written. In them, he fulfilled Archbishop Cullen's wish that he demonstrate how education in Ireland should be religious, in contrast to contemporary theories that left religion outside the walls of university learning. But he also set out to display the intrinsic worth of cultivating the mind, through a university which would offer a wide range of subjects, classical and literary as well as scientific, while also including the discipline of theology. His aim was the great enlargement of the human intellect, as it took in the whole circle and range of knowledge, and nothing less, viewed for its own sake. It would thereby learn, by a trained philosophical temper, to evaluate and compare the many aspects of reality, and reach out towards a comprehensive grasp of truth. The science of the mystery of God could no more be left out of that educational endeavour, than the intrinsic human desire to endeavour to understand all that makes up reality, and which overrides the more practical gaining of knowledge and skills for useful ends. And if the university be a Catholic one, then clearly the Church in some sense had a role to play, while allowing a true intellectual freedom to enquire, and to compare and evaluate.

The discourses are full of balance and nuance, every part depending on the other to build up Newman's vision of what he calls a 'liberal education'. Aspects of what he wrote are of course rooted in their time, and depend to an extent on his own university background, and on the controversies in England and Scotland then and in the past on learning and higher education. Again, viewed against the ever-increasing pressures to gain qualifications in view of a career, his unwavering belief that a university above all should cultivate learning for its own sake may seem impractical, while his necessary inclusion of theology within its range of disciplines is not often taken seriously. Yet what he says remains a courageous and classical articulation of what real education is about, where the whole circle of knowledge, and the mind's reaching towards its fullness, is promoted in a setting where each department of knowledge respects and takes into account the subject matter of the others, and no essential aspect of human understanding is left out.

Perhaps what remains most with readers is his delineation of the human product of such an education: a person ('a gentleman') of disciplined and wide-ranging intellect, clear-headed, courteous and noble in life, able to enter into the views of others, possibly having some religious belief, or if an unbeliever still a friend of religious toleration.[2] Yet the portrait is both attractive and frightening, because without true religious faith such refinement and learning is somehow empty, with pride and self-respect taking the place of true humility and love. There is indeed a 'religion of the world', as Newman had shown long ago, and outlines again now. It may happen to be the religious ideal of a civilised age, and in certain respects seem to be the equivalent of Christian faith. But such a religion, in a person of cultivated intellect and ethical character, is yet but a shallow reflection of that deeply-transforming one given by grace, as offered in the Gospel and through the ministration of the Church. Newman once again, in his *Discourses on the Scope and Nature of University Education*, comes back to the deep truths he had proclaimed in Oxford and as an Anglican educationalist and pastor.

Little enough from a practical point of view was to happen during 1853. Cullen had much else to occupy him at that time, with regard both to Church matters and the Irish politics of the time. He was running into difficulties with a number of the Irish bishops, and above all was being opposed by Archbishop MacHale, who although favouring Newman's appointment, would only support a university for Ireland alone and not one for the wider English-speaking world, and was against what he considered would be an English element running it. Newman wished to have a Vice-Rector appointed at some stage, but one of his own choosing, with whom he could work closely. Cullen ignored him on this, and imposed on him Dr James Taylor from Carlow College, but only as Secretary to the University, and who as it transpired had little dealings with Newman, being more a secretary to Cullen himself.

Cullen also bought, through the agency of Charles Bianconi, the fine Georgian house at 86 St Stephen's Green, which was to be called University House. Again this was presented as a *fait accompli*, Newman believing that a setting out in the neighbourhood of the city rather than in its centre would be better for the University. But interestingly, its location also brought up for him a vivid and living memory from the past – for nearby on St Stephen's Green was the residence of his old Oriel mentor, Richard Whately, Protestant Archbishop of Dublin since 1831. Newman had already enquired through an acquaintance if Whately would accept a visit from him, to be told firmly it was out of the question. And sometimes now he would find himself passing Whately on the street, but knowing he could not approach him.

The policy of Cullen in taking decisions with regard to the University without consulting him was of major concern to Newman. He was also made anxious, because his letters to the Archbishop on important matters were going unanswered. He felt he was being wrongfully left in the dark, and precious time was going by. But at least other things were engaging his attention, such as giving a course of lectures at the new Catholic Institute of Education in Liverpool, and preaching at the first diocesan synod in Birmingham. He was down in London too, in connection with the closure of King William

Street and the move of the Oratory out to the suburb of Brompton. And finally his own new Oratory church was opened on 22 November – significantly the Feast of St Cecilia, patroness of music, which had always been part of the Oratorian 'School of Christian Love'.

Newman, baffled by the Archbishop's silence and inactivity, began to wonder if he should resign at this stage. Perhaps too, as he questioned from the beginning, the fact of his being an Englishman was not helpful in the Ireland of that time. But in early 1854 matters at last began to move, with a Brief promised from the Pope to establish the University straightaway. In addition, he was informed by Wiseman that the Pope had agreed he should be a titular bishop to give him extra authority, putting him on a par with the Irish bishops responsible for the University, and not excluded from their deliberations. Word got out about this from Ullathorne, and friends sent congratulations and appropriate episcopal gifts (Ullathorne even treating him as a bishop, and calling him 'Right Reverend'). He gathered however from Cullen that he was lukewarm about the idea. What he did not know was that the Archbishop, behind the scenes, took immediate action in Rome to block his elevation – but no one took the trouble to inform Newman, leaving him in an embarrassing position when nothing happened, although later on very thankful the proposed honour had not come his way.

In early February he set out once again on another of his many journeys to Dublin, but believing now it was make-or-break time for setting up the University. It was the worst winter in Ireland since 1814 and Newman was coping with one of the recurrent severe colds that were often his lot. He managed the train journey along the exposed North Wales coast, and then 'a very stiff passage' across the Irish Sea. He was determined to meet as many bishops as possible, to elicit their support.

In Dublin, nearly everyone he wanted to consult was either engaged or away. But he succeeded in meeting the Jesuit Provincial, Fr John Curtis, 'a man of great character and experience' in his estimation, who told him very clearly that there was no hope for the University. Ireland with its poverty did not have the class of youths for it, he said. As for the 'gentleman class', who wanted a proper degree, they sent their sons to Trinity College, and the 'upper class', theirs to the English universities. As for evening classes, he said there were no youths in Dublin to fill them, 'unless I looked to the persons who frequented concerts etc. – men, women, and children'. And the Provincial ended by advising him to go the Bishop and say: 'Don't attempt the University; give up the idea.'[3] Coming away from him, Newman however was still determined to go ahead, although conceding in a letter to Ambrose St John that Fr Curtis 'is not a bird of good omen as regards the University'.

Stiffening his resolve, in fact, he even thought momentarily of possibly heading for America, to visit 'the *principal* Catholic cities from New York to New Orleans', to get support. But instead he held to his plan of calling on the bishops, and so started off by heading south on a 'circuit' by train, to the bishops at Kilkenny, Carlow, Waterford, Cork, Thurles and Limerick. Virtually everywhere he met kindness, but not necessarily the support he was looking for.

In letters back to Birmingham he recounted his adventures, as for instance how the cabman at Kilkenny station, despite the instructions given him, deposited his English passenger at the Protestant bishop's palace close by the beautiful medieval St Canice's Cathedral, leaving him to find his own way to Dr Walsh, incumbent of the rival and still unfinished St Mary's. Down in Cork, Bishop Delany was cool towards him; naturally so, since with a Queen's College already on his doorstep, which he thought would do for Catholics very well, he was hostile to what Newman represented. But Archbishop Slattery of Thurles he found to be 'a most pleasing, taking man – mild, tender and broken'. As for Bishop Ryan of Limerick: 'He is a man I like very much – a down-right, honest, bluff person – very hearty and very positive ... He is the cleverest bishop I have met, and certainly to me the kindest.' Like Fr Curtis, Bishop Ryan again was very honest with him, telling him to expect the failure of an enterprise which lacked government support – and a failure, he hastened to add, which would not be Newman's fault.

He had intended to go further, to visit the western bishops, including MacHale in Tuam, then travel across the Midlands, and into the northern dioceses. But he had another severe cold now, which had worsened. He did not feel up to the prospect of travelling onwards from Limerick, the railway to Ennis and beyond not yet opened, and having to face instead tedious coach journeys by road in the severe conditions. So he had to cancel his plans, while aware that personal dealings with as many bishops as possible was vital to his role as Rector. Many of the others he would meet in time, either in Dublin or in Maynooth.

Back in Dublin, and as he recovered, he had contact with his old friend Dr Russell, now Vice-President of Maynooth, who likewise held out little hope for the University. If was as if, he felt, in Fr Curtis, Bishop Ryan and Dr Russell he was hearing the voice of the late Dr Murray of Dublin speaking to him. But still he went ahead, making contact with a range of people who might become tutors, lecturers and professors, and looking out for the lease of more property to house the University's institutions and residences. In April the Papal Brief finally arrived, approving him as Rector. In May the bishops met to make necessary arrangements, and decreed, as Newman requested, the establishment of five faculties: Theology, Law, Medicine, Philosophy and Letters, and Science. Then, on 4 June, Pentecost Sunday, in the Metropolitan Church of St Mary (soon to be Dublin's Pro-Cathedral) he was officially installed as Rector of the Catholic University of Ireland. And, for a while, it seemed as if matters would turn out well after all.

At this time, he published a series of letters in Henry Wilberforce's *Catholic Standard*, on Britain's entry into what became known as the Crimean War. Coming after forty years of peace, the war was to have a traumatic effect on people at home. Under the heading of 'Who's to Blame?' and using his old pseudonym 'Catholicus', he wrote of the needlessness of Britain's involvement, in taking, along with France, the side of the Turks against the Russians. 'We have enveloped ourselves in illusions and shams, as John Bull always does,' he told Catherine Froude.

He had also been travelling in England. In March he was in London, to attend the opening of the new church at the Brompton Oratory. In May he went to Stone, in Staffordshire, where Margaret

Hallahan and her Dominican community had moved, to preach at the opening of their church. He had promised Mother Margaret he would do so, and would not let her down, 'though I have to come from Connemara or the Giant's Causeway'. He was in good spirits the rest of that summer, spending much of the time back in Birmingham, and into the autumn in Dublin yet again, borrowing a holiday house – 'Mount Salus', above the village of Dalkey – for his own community's use. He walked a lot while there, loving the view over Killiney Bay, while also working away at preparations for the opening of the University in November.

All the year, he was in the business of recruiting staff. Among these was the great scholar Eugene O'Curry, who accepted the chair of Archaeology and Irish History, with Newman later attending all his lectures, funding his publications and having an Irish-language type cast for him. Denis Florence McCarthy, the Young Ireland poet, who was recommended by Dr David Moriarty (now Coadjutor to the Bishop of Kerry), agreed to be Professor of Poetry. Others included John O'Hagan as Lecturer in Political Economy, William Sullivan Professor of Chemistry, Edward Butler Professor of Mathematics, Terence Flanagan Professor of Civil Engineering, and Henry Hennessy Professor of Natural Philosophy (Physics). Keen to have the distinguished convert, Aubrey de Vere, in the University, he eventually persuaded him to become Professor of Political and Social Science. Where possible, he wanted a lay staff, but looked for clerics where appropriate – travelling for instance to the new Jesuit Theologate at St Beuno's in North Wales to persuade Dr Edmund O'Reilly SJ, formerly of Maynooth College, to become Professor of Dogmatic Theology. And Dr Patrick Leahy of St Patrick's College, Thurles, who was now appointed by the bishops as his Vice-Rector – against his repeated wish that the position should be of his own choosing, and moreover a layman – became Professor of Exegetics. He even tried, but in vain, to entice Ignaz Döllinger over from Munich, to be either Professor of Ecclesiastical History, or else be one of a distinguished panel who would give occasional series of lectures.

Although Cullen was agreeable with the notion of a predominantly lay staff, he nevertheless was becoming critical of Newman. He thought he was engaging too large a staff at this early stage, all having to be paid (albeit low salaries by any reckoning) out of the limited funds available. But Newman felt it was right to have a wide-ranging and capable academic staff at the beginning, which would give the University the prestige it required, and draw good students. 'The supply must be before the demand,' he said. As for the finances, he wanted a committee of laymen to take charge of them, on a professional basis, and which would have met Cullen's objection that he was spending too much money. He knew that important laymen were holding back substantial contributions, and precisely because the finances were in episcopal hands. But to the bishops the idea of a lay finance committee was out of the question, as it would have given the laity a major say in the running of the University.

The extra buildings which went to form the University's nucleus included part of Dr Quinn's school at 16 Harcourt Street, which retained its name as St Laurence's House. Shortly before the opening of the University Newman acquired the lease of 6 Harcourt Street, which he called St Mary's House, which he began to fit out as his own residence, with a chapel, and other rooms available to students and lecturers. University House itself, at 86 St Stephen's Green, became known as St Patrick's. Newman had also acquired the Cecilia Street Medical School, although it would be a year before it opened again under the auspices of the University. Other matters of course engaged the necessary attention of Rector and staff members, such as drawing up statutes, discussion of curricula, and even the drafting of examination papers.

And very quietly, on Friday, 3 November 1854, Feast of St Malachy, the doors of the Catholic University, at 86 St Stephen's Green, opened for the first students. There were about twenty in all, with Newman hosting a reception for them and their lecturers the following Sunday. Most of the small intake was naturally from the Irish middle classes, and they were lodged in the three different Houses. Forty more were pledged to come, which they duly did in time, and there was even word from Cullen (in Rome at this time) that American families were intending to send their children, to be under Newman.

He had launched the *Catholic University Gazette*, a weekly publication with news and articles, in the summer, and now there was a series of inaugural lectures, with the first given by himself on 'Christianity and Letters'. In addition, evening lectures were being planned, for 'mechanics' and others who could not avail of the day courses. As for degrees, he felt the University's granting them in its own right would lead to the public's recognition and endorsement, while Rome would allow Pontifical ones to those taking courses in the Sacred Sciences. He hoped that as a result there would be a full government recognition of them. The project was therefore finally under way, and Newman could be forgiven for a sense of relief and revived hope when he headed home to Birmingham at Christmas – while also wondering, as he had confided to Ambrose St John back in the summer, how he could continue to find the personal resources for work in the two places.

NOTES

1. *SVO*, pp. 163–82.
2. *Idea*, pp. 208–11.
3. *AW*, p. 323.

— CHAPTER 7 —

Between Two Worlds

RETURNING TO DUBLIN in the New Year of 1855, Newman was still able to summon up energy to meet a series of issues requiring his attention. But he was happy, nevertheless, to let the academic and administrative staff get on with the main business of the University. From a pastoral point of view, he was also on a daily basis looking after the students in his residence – which included a number from England, Scotland and France – running what by all accounts was a cheerful household, and where for himself personally the centre of it all was the chapel and the Blessed Sacrament. Cullen however, from reports he was receiving, was less than impressed by what he considered was the Rector's lack of control over discipline in general. Newman's experience of real university life, after all, had been very different from Cullen's background in clerical and Roman establishments, and the young men were simply being encouraged to both be themselves and be mature. And Edward Butler, for instance, who had acted as Newman's working Vice-Rector early on, held the view that the Irish bishops did not really understand what a university should be, and could only envisage a kind of glorified seminary for the laity.

But more serious differences between Cullen and Newman were now emerging. Among the academic staff, some of the ablest men engaged by Newman were ex-Young Irelanders, and included

O'Curry, O'Hagan and Sullivan, as well as Denis Florence McCarthy. Cullen had a rooted animadversion against the Young Irelanders in general, who had been looking for national independence, and were responsible for the small 1848 insurrection in Ballingarry. He believed they were as much anti-clerical as their contemporaries in Mazzini's Young Italy, who had driven the Pope temporarily out of Rome during the 1848 revolution there. Some of them in turn, along with Archbishop MacHale, and Frederick Lucas, tended to regard Cullen as a 'Castle Bishop', too closely aligned with the English government's policies towards Ireland at that time.

While he had not blocked Newman's appointees, Cullen still told him, in a letter from Rome in January 1855, to avoid association with agitators against himself – 'I trust you will make every exertion to keep the University free from all Young Irelandism.' Newman in reply however, while hoping that politics would be kept out of the University, said of the Young Irelanders he knew: 'All I know is, that they are admirable persons now, and, I am sure, would show nothing of the spirit of which your Grace complains so justly.' In particular, he would not concur with Cullen's negative view of Frederick Lucas: 'I know him and respect him highly', he said in the same letter, although conceding that Lucas might possibly be extreme in some of his criticisms.[1] Statements like these, naturally, were further alienating Cullen from him. Still Newman would be unrepentant. Later on he would say he was never sorry he looked for the assistance of the former Young Irelanders. For him, as he saw it in retrospect, it really had to do with how the laity generally were being looked upon by the clerical authorities: they 'were treated like good little boys – were told to shut their eyes and open their mouths, and take what we give to them.'[2]

During the next summer holidays Newman diverted himself by resuming work on another novel, which he had started in 1848. He had begun it after finishing *Loss and Gain*, but only now found the time and inspiration to really get down to work on it. Published in 1856 as *Callista: A Tale of the Third Century*, it recounts the conversion of its Greek heroine Callista, with quite a depth of psychological and human insight, and offering valuable points of comparison with contemporary experiences of conversion in England. The detailing of

Callista's journey of conscience is quite profound, and has echoes of Newman's own agonising journey, while also drawing on the understanding of faith outlined in the *Oxford University Sermons*.

Newman had also managed to find a place for a number of English converts on his staff. On the academic side, they included T.W. Allies who was Lecturer in the Philosophy of History, and Robert Ornsby (whose advice he especially valued), Professor of Greek and Latin. Thomas Arnold, son of his late famed opponent, would become Professor of English Literature. But it was another of his convert acquaintances who would make the most significant contribution both to the University and to Dublin. John Hungerford Pollen, who like others including Aubrey de Vere had been deeply influenced by Newman's preaching in Oxford, lost his inheritance on becoming a Catholic in 1852. Having a talent for painting and sketching, Newman was able to offer him the Professorship of Fine Arts, which included the post of architect and decorator. From the beginning, and understandably so from his experience of St Mary's at Oxford, Newman had wanted a University Church, which would be at the very centre of Dublin's new seat of learning. He now felt he could set about its building, having a shared vision with Pollen as to what was needed, and managed to acquire a site, in the garden at the back, next door to University House in St Stephen's Green.

With Pollen's design to hand in June 1855, work went ahead quickly, and the University Church was opened on 1 May 1856, Ascension Thursday. Substantially complete, a few months more were needed to accomplish everything within it. As Newman said later in life, his plan had been to 'build a large barn, and decorate it in the style of a basilica, with Irish marbles and copies of standard pictures'. A jewel of Irish craftsmanship, made from Irish materials, and enhanced by Pollen's own painting, it is the nearest Dublin would come to an Italianate basilica, with Byzantine features. In the apse is the central figure of Mary as *Sedes Sapientiae*, the 'Seat of Wisdom', for it was to her that Newman as rector had entrusted the whole project of the University.

The building of the University Church was one of the high points of Newman's time in Dublin. He was delighted with what Pollen had achieved. Pollen himself, and his new young wife Maria, never forgot the happiness of their times in Dublin spent in the company of Newman. And at the heart of it all was Newman's abiding consciousness of how his 'large barn' was mainly paid for: with the money left over from the many subscriptions to his legal expenses at the Achilli trial, coming from the poor Catholic people of Ireland itself, as well as from Britain and many other countries.

Just after the opening of the Church, for the Feast of St Monica, in early May 1856, Newman preached on 'Intellect, the Instrument of Religious Training', where he drew from the example of Monica's concern for the spiritual and human welfare of her son, St Augustine. In all, he would preach on eight occasions in the University Church. His written texts, published in *Sermons Preached on Various Occasions*, are significant, in that they continue in the vein of his preaching at Oxford. One of them, entitled 'Waiting for Christ', is a reworked version of the great Anglican sermon, 'Watching'. Another, 'Dispositions for Faith', is the Anglican 'Faith without Sight' rewritten, where the original reflections, on the role of conscience in coming to faith, are developed significantly. The sermon, 'Omnipotence in Bonds' reads as a beautiful Christmas homily, although preached after Epiphany 1857, and equal in its way to any preached in Oxford. The final two, 'St Paul's Characteristic Gift' and 'St Paul's Gift of Sympathy', preached in early 1857, have special reference to the aims of the University, where human attainments require the purifying and sublimating blessings of grace. The high quality of these sermons is striking, and they show how, with suitable liturgy, good preaching was intended by Newman to be at the heart of the University's life.

But the two worlds he was living in was having its effect. Active as he was on the Dublin scene, Newman found that the various issues affecting the Oratory in England could not be avoided and so often required his attention. The Oratory after all was his first loyalty, and from the start of his involvement in Ireland he knew he could only give a limited number of years to the University. He was continually travelling those long rail journeys, and braving the Irish Sea, going to and fro between England and Ireland. Now, as it turned out, with the

University established and its daily management in the hands of a fine staff, he had to turn more and more to the Oratory, with perhaps its very future at stake, or at least to his mind its essential composition. It was natural that some in Ireland could not appreciate his dilemma, especially Cullen. But Newman, even if he felt torn to some extent, was certain about where his main responsibilities lay.

The difficulties between the two Oratories had continued. As well as the manner in which Faber's group had been thrust upon him initially, and which had required much sorting out, there had been another underlying problem for Newman. While as an Anglican he had been the leader and inspiration to these younger men who were now Oratorians, the fact of their becoming Catholics had changed considerably how he was seen by them. As beginners in learning Catholic ways, and on the same level with the older Newman therefore, these former disciples had taken more eagerly to the Italian and devotional practices then in vogue, with those in London being in the limelight of Catholic life and ministry. Newman by contrast had been left behind in these matters, they felt. And in time they would begin to think of him as somehow not Catholic enough. Paradoxically, still revering him to a degree, they craved to have him as an authoritarian and father figure, a need which was beyond him to supply.

For indeed in the Church then authoritarianism was in the air, with an increasing focus on the mystique and person of the Pope. The times were uncertain, in the wake of the revolutionary year of 1848, and Ultramontane ('beyond the mountains') loyalty by the northern European countries to Rome's jurisdiction was seen by many as the answer to the threats of the age. As for the Pope himself, what had been his own mild flirting with liberalism had come to an end when he fled into exile in 1848, from the brief Roman Republic of Garibaldi and Mazzini – and henceforth he was to set the Papacy, in heroic isolation, against the progressive ideas and political developments of the nineteenth century. Battle lines were beginning to be drawn, then, between Ultramontane and more liberal Catholics, and Newman's place in it all would become a fascinating and prophetic one. But at this early stage a more domestic version of the drama was being acted out, which would leave him quite seriously damaged and misunderstood.

In October 1855 Newman learned that the London Oratory unilaterally had applied to the Congregation of Propaganda in Rome for a change of the English Oratory Rule, which forbade the hearing of nuns' confessions. This was a work increasingly being undertaken by the London Oratory, and in addition by Bernard Dalgairns (he had taken the name Bernard as an Oratorian), who was back in Birmingham after being part of the London community in its early years. The reason for not allowing this outside work of confession, or spiritual direction, was that it took members away from the Oratory itself, which was meant to be the abiding centre of their apostolate (Newman himself only allowed to be away in Dublin because of 'grave necessity'). Newman however was concerned about what he believed was a serious point of principle, in the one house acting to get a dispensation from the Rule – revised by himself at the Pope's behest, who had given him the responsibility to bring it to England and oversee – without consulting him on the matter. He was also upset when the dispensation was granted by Propaganda, and by its wording seeming to apply to both houses.

Letters passed to and fro, between Dublin and Birmingham and London, leading to a hardening of attitudes rather than resolution. Newman feared that London wished to be considered the pre-eminent Oratory in England, and indeed when the Rescript came from Rome permitting relaxation of the Rule, it referred to Faber as 'Provost of the Oratorians of England'. Wiseman was drawn into the controversy, Newman consulting him on how he might approach the Congregation of Propaganda, to clear up matters satisfactorily. Faber of course in London had easier access to Wiseman, and it was during correspondence between them that Wiseman urged on Faber a soothing of Newman's 'noble wounded spirit', perhaps using these words mainly to help Faber towards reconciliation. The opposite was what tended to happen, however, and later Faber excitedly reported to the Cardinal the fiction that Newman was bent on introducing a 'generalate' over the English Oratory. Wiseman himself in turn became alienated, when he proposed to dedicate a work of his jointly to Newman and Faber, and Newman responded by asking if the Birmingham community be associated with his own name. 'The insolence of Dr Newman', or 'the fellow', he was reported to have said. Newman, far away, was helpless in all of this, and angry because he knew his private letters were being passed about, including his recent response to Wiseman being casually shown to Faber.

Newman went to Rome with Ambrose St John, starting out on St Stephen's Day 1855, to try to clear up the matter. They visited various Oratories on the way, not knowing that Faber had sent ahead letters to them all and to Rome, containing the claim of Newman's supposed ambition for a generalate. Although they were kindly received in Rome, and Newman's rightful but limited authority in England confirmed, the secret letters from the Brompton Oratory had in fact weakened the regard in which he was held there. And mistrust deepened further in London afterwards, Brompton further able to influence the Cardinal, and some of the prominent Catholic laity in London, against Newman. It came down, as they saw it, to Newman's sensitive feelings, and they fancied that no effort on their part would gain his forgiveness over their wounding him. For Newman, it was nothing of the sort, but about a matter of principle, on which he was standing firm. It was about honesty and transparency in their dealings with one another, where in the end they might agree to differ. In fact, they were irrevocably in the process of becoming completely independent. Two of the Brompton men, Stanton and Hutchison, went to Rome in July 1856 to petition for a separate Brief, looking for this independence. Newman had already asked for this himself, only to be told it was not necessary. Stanton and Hutchison however were more successful, and got the Brief they required. But what is sad is revealed in their letters back to London, where they call Newman 'the Serpent', and later 'Il Babbo' ('Daddy'), the nickname shared with them by Cardinal Barnabò in Propaganda.

So the Oratories went their own way, Brompton heading into the frontline of Ultramontane enthusiasm, and Faber, despite prolonged bouts of illness and absences, writing a popular series of devotional books, and in demand as a preacher. Birmingham, hidden away, had little to show for itself to the wide world, apart from perhaps

Newman's work in Dublin. And Dalgairns, who never settled in Birmingham, and felt that there was a lack of St Philip Neri's authentic spirit there, went back down to the London scene. In fact, good work in different spheres was done by both Oratories. But the gossip in London circles continued the slander that Newman was sensitive, resentful and impossible to deal with. He for his part asked his community to keep silent about the conflict, not wishing to expose what he believed was Faber's double-dealing, or to undermine the general high regard in which the London Oratorians were held.

All this, while travelling to and from Dublin, helping to keep the University on a steady course and enabling it to develop. A Rectorial Council of faculty deans was established, as was the Academic Senate. Lectures in the School of Engineering were begun. The Historical, Literary and Aesthetical Society was founded, for debating and discussion – and which, as the noted Literary and Historical Society, continued in University College, Dublin. Particular efforts were made to get the best possible talent for the Medical School, and in this regard Newman was eminently successful, with the Royal College of Surgeons recognising the courses and staff, and eventually too other licensing bodies in England and Scotland. It was opened on 2 November 1855, and a month later Newman gave a lecture there, on 'Christianity and Physical Science'. At the end of its first year, he would write in his report to the bishops: 'Did our efforts towards the foundation of a Catholic University issue in nothing beyond the establishment of a first-rate Catholic School of Medicine in the metropolis, as it has already done, they would have met with sufficient reward'.

But the question of recognition of the University's degrees was a real one. There were many who felt that public endorsement of what the University granted was simply not enough, and would deter students coming who wanted and needed state-recognised qualifications. A charter from the government was required, as many of the University staff saw clearly, and Cullen, and indeed Newman himself. He was in any case at this time being worn down once more by what he believed were Cullen's delaying tactics, his failure again to answer letters, and his inability to trust him or indeed virtually anyone else. His repeated representations, such as to have a lay finance committee, which would raise much-need funds as well as responsibly supervise expenditure, were again rebuffed. The clerical control being exercised, and the disregard of the laity, left Newman deeply discouraged, and incidentally too fearing for the future of the Irish Church. He began to realise more clearly that the University was turning out to be an institution just for Ireland, and not the beacon and centre of learning he had hoped it would be for a wider world. And he had all the worry and trouble of the Oratorian conflict in England.

Still there were further good developments. In 1857 the excellent journal *Atlantis* was founded, which was intended to display the talent of the staff, especially from the Faculty of Science, in learned articles. The innovative evening classes, which had started in 1854, but were suspended soon after because of lack of support, were now restarted in April 1858. This time they were very successful, the professors throwing themselves into the work with enthusiasm, with courses of high quality being offered, which could lead to degrees – and as a result nearly three hundred young men were eventually enrolled.

Meanwhile, with religious tests abolished in Oxford and Cambridge, and the prospect of Catholics attending these, Newman began to admit that Catholic halls or colleges in existing universities might be a part of the way forward after all. In his heart, he had come clearly now to the realisation that he could do no more in Ireland. In April 1856 he warned Archbishop Cullen that he intended to retire in July of the following year, when his original leave of absence from the Oratory would expire. He sent out letters to all the bishops to that effect. He felt thwarted and undermined by Cullen. He was frustrated too by MacHale's lack of cooperation – the only friendly intermediary between them, Frederick Lucas, having died prematurely, broken in spirit and in impoverished circumstances in late 1855. Matters were not helped when the Vice-Rector, Dr Leahy, departed to be Archbishop of Cashel in June 1857. Newman, again wanting a Vice-Rector of his own choosing, and a layman, hoped that he could get Edward Butler for the post. But that could not be agreed to, and only after interminable delays – and after his own final departure – did a reluctant Dr James Gartlan, Rector of the Irish College at Salamanca, arrive on the scene, and then have the job of acting Rector in Newman's place.

Cullen had remained critical of Newman, and complained continually about him, especially in Rome, lamenting in particular his frequent absences, which he felt had held back the progress of the University. But despite his criticisms, he still wanted to hold on to him, fearing quite rightly that Newman's departure would seriously lessen its chances of future success. He had hoped, like Newman himself for a time, that an Irish Oratory could be founded, but with the expectation that it would have kept his Rector in Dublin. He even went at one point to Birmingham, appearing before Newman in a nervous and distressed state, to plead earnestly with him to stay on. Newman however was determined to go, wanting to leave in Irish hands what he believed now was simply an Irish concern, and anyway disenchanted with a lack of interest in England for what had been his wider vision of the University. He was utterly fatigued, and could do no more. It was a work requiring the energy of someone twenty years younger, he thought.

Newman ceased taking his salary in early 1858, remaining on that year in the capacity of non-resident Rector, but contributing articles to the *Atlantis*. At the start of the next academic year, at the beginning of November, he was present to give three inaugural lectures, on 'Discipline of Mind' to the evening classes, on 'Literature' to the School of Philosophy and Letters, and on 'Christianity and Medical Science' to the Medical School. He then finally crossed to England and although he personally resigned soon after, officially his resignation was not accepted until 10 August 1859. He would maintain a great interest in the University, and be in correspondence about it, for years ahead.

At first, his ending in Ireland left him with a sense of acute disappointment over the whole venture. Tired out, and also personally affected by the partial unravelling of his Oratorian dream back home, he seems to have lost for a while something of his usual buoyancy in troubled times. He remained quite bleak in his assessment of the 'silent, impenetrable' Cullen, and the negative MacHale as well, even if he had sometimes felt sympathy with Cullen's wider political and ecclesiastical troubles. Some of his friends gave out to him about his complaining, but he felt his 'croaking' was no different from that of Job, and Jeremiah, and the Psalmist. 'To let out one's feeling is a great relief, and I don't think an unlawful one,' he said to Ambrose St John. Yet fundamentally he never regretted having taken up the invitation to come over to Ireland and help as best he could.

In 1873 Newman would combine his university discourses with the other lectures he gave in Dublin, together with some articles, to make his still invaluable book *The Idea of a University*. As for his hope for the Catholic University itself, initiated by Cullen, and envisaged as a great Irish centre of learning for the English-speaking world, it was certainly a valiant aspiration, but hardly destined to succeed, especially considering the state of post-Famine Ireland at that time. He conceded as much later: 'I was a poor innocent,' he wrote, 'as regards the actual state of things in Ireland when I went there, and did not care to think about it, for I relied on the word of the Pope, but from the event I am led to think it not rash to say that I knew as much about Ireland as he did.'[3] Yet something good had been started, which would show itself in time. The University would certainly struggle after he had left, missing his active and inspirational presence. In 1882 University College was instituted, in effect taking the place of the Catholic University, and situated in what was formerly Newman's University House on Stephen's Green. It was one of the constituent colleges of the Royal University, an examining and degree-awarding institution. In turn it would evolve into the present-day University College Dublin. So a link goes back from today to what had modestly but heroically originated in those far-off days of the 1850s.

Newman had made good friends in Ireland, including among the clergy, many of whom would keep in contact. But it was the lay staff above all in the University who valued him. John O'Hagan, his Professor of Political Economy, aware of how he had been treated by Cullen and MacHale, said that even if there were some in Ireland who never understood or appreciated him, it was quite the opposite where the Irish lay professors were concerned: 'We have felt that you only wanted power and freedom of action to make the institution march.'[4] And Eugene O'Curry, in the preface to his *Lectures on the Manuscript Materials of Ancient Irish History*, published later in 1861, would call to mind Newman's constant attendance at his lectures, his kindly sympathy and active continual encouragement. He would also testify to Newman's 'warmly felt and oft-expressed sympathy with Erin, her wrongs and her hopes, as well as her history'.

On his own reckoning, he had crossed the Irish Sea fifty-six times in the work he had undertaken in Ireland. Time and time again he had travelled the lengthy rail journey between Birmingham and Holyhead, on the famous Irish Mail route between Stafford, Crewe and Chester, along the Welsh coast and over the great Stephenson bridge spanning the Menai Straits to the Isle of Anglesea and Holyhead. Then there had been the crossings to and from Kingstown, summer and winter, some calm, but some on a rough sea with the Mail steamer pitching and rolling, and Newman either having a berth below or else on the open deck, stretched out on a bench if he could find one, sometimes glad of the cold fresh winds when feeling sick. It had all been part of his experience in visiting Ireland, and where he often felt overwhelmed by kindness, welcomed even as an Englishman, because of his faith and commitment, and despite the history of his native country's dominance there. Desolate always leaving Birmingham, as he had admitted once to Edward Caswall, he had been 'thrown among strangers' in Ireland, who took him in and mostly valued him, while in return he had given all he could. And now he had finally gone back to Birmingham and to his own.

NOTES

1. *LD*, XVI, p. 359.
2. *AW*, p. 328.
3. *AW*, p. 320.
4. *LD*, XVIII, 483n.

— CHAPTER 8 —

Dark Days and Faithfulness

WITHOUT DOUBT, THE Oratorian way was at the heart of Newman's own life as a Catholic. After prayer and study he had entered into its spirit while in Rome, and taken upon himself to live it out, and promote it on his return to England. Of course, the great change for him had been his reception into the 'one Fold of the Redeemer' in 1845, and his full-hearted acceptance of its worship and its teachings. But within that, concretely, his own living in the companionship of like-minded Oratorians was vital to him. He loved the spirit of St Philip Neri, and so often referred to him in public, as for instance in 'The Second Spring', at the end of his University Discourses, and in his Dublin sermons. The Oratory, in a very important sense of the word, was his home.

For Newman, familial ties and close companionship had been vital and intrinsic parts of his own well-being. It could even be said that his own calling as an Anglican to an unmarried life, and his continuing to live that ideal as a Catholic, depended not just on his deep sense of being always before God, but also on the surrounding kind warmth of companions and friends. He was not without personal feeling and needs, but in the right kind of human setting he could centre his innermost self on God, and devote his energies to the Gospel and its Catholic manifestation. The Oratory community, as one without vows, depended on the bonds of 'human affection' and Christian charity, to keep it together, and under the benign guidance of its Superior. There was a certain difference of emphasis in its operation, compared to that of the religious orders, which were more strongly organised and directed. It was a way which suited Newman, and other converts with a similar background to his own, and provided them with an environment in which they could both find their place and offer a rich and much-needed service within the growing world of English Catholicism.

Naturally then, the conflicts which had originated in the Oratory were to him a cause of deep pain. They arose out of a particular set of circumstances, as we have seen. Idealistic and eager younger men, as well as Faber himself, who would do much good in their way, had got it into their heads that the older Newman was out of touch, set on dominance, and they latched onto the lie of his 'wounded feelings' to avoid facing some real issues which needed sorting. Rather than risk what might have been admittedly the catharsis of growth into truth and mutual respect, the more convenient route of prejudice was followed, leading to sad estrangement.

Newman was also disappointed when the prospect of other Oratorian foundations faded, and which in some measure resulted from their own divisions. There had been a hope for one in Leeds, when he received there a number of clergy and laymen from Pusey's foundation of St Saviour's, but in the end nothing came of it. Other hopes had been for such as Dublin and Liverpool, and also especially for London's East End, among the Irish there – this latter possibility ended by the Brief obtained by Hutchison and Stanton in Rome, which forbade the foundation of another London Oratory. And, as well, Newman had felt that his long absences in Dublin had been detrimental to the Birmingham community. They needed his presence, just as he needed their companionship and support. Now at last the group, properly together, would have the best possible opportunity to live out their vocation, centred on their house and church, with pastoral responsibility for a large area, and in addition being at the service of the wider Church in whatever way seemed best.

One avenue of work seemed to open up, when in August 1857 Wiseman wrote to Newman to say the bishops at the Westminster Synod of 1855 had entrusted him with supervision over a new translation of the Bible. Wondering about the delay in telling him, and having checked that this in fact was the bishops' wish, Newman started making arrangements for such a large venture, writing to numerous relevant people for advice and suggestions, and beginning to work out a team of translators. It seemed a timely project, as the old Rheims-Douay version, although revised by Bishop Challoner in the eighteenth century, was generally considered out of date by now. Then it transpired that a new American translation was separately in progress, with the hierarchy there naturally seeing no point to a second endeavour, but willing to have Newman's cooperation in theirs. Newman found out about this when Wiseman passed on their letters to him, but with no comment. In the end, as if to recapitulate the Dublin experience, Newman was once again simply left in the dark, with no further communication from Wiseman, and the initial work and expense coming to nothing.

A more successful undertaking was the Oratory school, which was founded at the request of influential lay friends, and intended for 'the education of the sons of gentlemen'. This, Newman believed, would fulfil a real need for a smaller Catholic public school, catering for converts who wanted their sons educated after the manner of the English public schools they had known, but with a good deal of care, and with less of the strictness found in some of the existing Catholic establishments. It would involve not the whole Oratorian community, but only Newman himself, and a lay staff, and Fr Nicholas Darnell as headmaster, who had been one of Faber's Wilfridians but had remained in the Birmingham Oratory. Much of what the Oratorians had done up to now was at the service of the poor. This new work however would fulfil the direction in the original Papal Brief, personally inserted in it by the Pope himself, that the Oratorians should especially direct their labours towards the more highly educated class of people. Launched in May 1859, and with a new building erected for it soon after, the school grew steadily and had seventy boys by 1862.

As for the community itself, there were both reasons for satisfaction and continuing cause for concern. Disappointingly, none of the laybrothers were able to persevere, and all had departed by now. The episode with Bernard Dalgairns back in their midst had been a disturbing one as well. Restless in himself, and governed by an intense and unreal form of French spirituality, Dalgairns could not help being continually critical of the mundane Birmingham Oratorians. He believed that even Newman, 'the old gentleman', had no interior life, no ardour for souls. When he had gone, Newman admitted to his companions that he had not handled the young man well: 'I am quite deficient in what the Life of St Ignatius (which we are now reading in our refectory) ascribes to that great saint so justly, the art of government … I think another person *could* have managed Fr Bernard.'[1] It had been a relief then when he returned to Faber and the more fervent London Oratory, and had done so with Newman's full blessing.

Among other things, Dalgairns had complained that the Birmingham community was an idle one – when in fact quite the opposite was the case. Stanislas Flanagan, the only born Catholic among the group, worked tirelessly, particularly in the working-class area of Smethwick, while also being responsible for the Catholics in the workhouse. All the rest were also busy with the church and parish, with the poor schools, the prison and an orphanage. Overwork led to health problems among them, Newman himself having to see a London specialist, Stanislas being diagnosed with the dreaded tuberculosis, and Henry Bittleston, who had joined them in 1850, getting seriously ill with pleurisy. Stanislas was sent off abroad, and eventually recuperated. Henry Bittleston nearly died, but having gained enough strength went away to join Stanislas for a long period. In addition, Ambrose St John was a severe asthmatic, subject to frightening attacks at times. Newman himself took over Stanislas's job as novicemaster, and eventually there was one who would persevere, Henry Ryder, who had been a student with him in Dublin. He would become Fr Ignatius Ryder, a good theologian, and Superior after Newman's death.

The others needed good time off in the summer of 1859, Newman covering for them, and sometimes finding himself alone in the house, overseeing alterations to it, and dealing with visitors. He had no proper break himself – the reason being that he was personally quite impoverished now. Only later, when his circumstances were found out, did others ensure he could afford a proper holiday. At least he could go away occasionally overnight to their own little villa house at Rednal, some eight miles out, on a wooded slope at the edge of the beautiful Lickey Hills. The house had been finished in the summer of 1855, and had its own piece of land with cemetery attached. But Newman did not sleep there until the remains of Joseph Gordon and Aloysius Boland had been re-interred close by. He looked forward to going out, and being involved in practical work, fencing the property, planting trees, and in addition looking after 'Charlie', a pony presented by Hope-Scott.

The church itself had been enlarged by this time, with the roof raised, and an aisle added, to cater for the increasing numbers. More improvements would take place in the years ahead. In it, Newman once more became a parish confessor, having been off the rota during the Dublin years. He was nervous and reluctant at first, feeling he had not always been helpful to penitents in Alcester Street. An important ministry, it required a special gift of listening and understanding, as people valued both the sacrament itself and good words of advice and guidance offered. But once he started again he got used to it, and took his turn with the other Fathers all the years until he was made a cardinal. Some people who had come to him before in Alcester Street now began turning up again, to become regular penitents. 'Old Mrs Brennan has found me out', he mentioned once, although noticing that while many factory boys had come in the past, now it was mostly girls and older people. And the other usual church duties came his way, not always with unqualified success, as when he 'made a hash of it' during a baptism, running out of water during the extended blessing in the ritual then – and finding out only afterwards that both parents were Protestants. Other duties of course included preaching, as well as singing the High Masses.

The same year of 1859, however, was a significant one for other reasons, when he was drawn into a wider field of action – and with disastrous consequences for his standing in Rome. In January there appeared in the *Rambler* magazine an article by Scott Nasmyth Stokes, a Catholic Inspector of Schools, advocating cooperation with the Royal Commission on elementary education, as opposed to the bishops' policy of non-cooperation. Started in 1848 by John Moore Capes, a married clergy convert, the *Rambler* was a magazine of high quality, intended to take up 'all subjects of literary, philosophical and moral interest'. Recently Sir John Acton had become part owner, and Richard Simpson the main editor. Acton was a young Catholic aristocrat, aged only twenty-five, but already a first-rate historian who had studied under Ignaz Döllinger in Munich. Richard Simpson was another married clergyman convert, who was then writing a biography of the Elizabethan Jesuit martyr Edmund Campion, and would become a noted Shakespearean scholar. Already before the January article, the bishops were unhappy with the *Rambler*, because of its straying into some theological matters, and Newman himself advising Acton to keep theology out of it. The article on education however particularly annoyed Wiseman, who proposed to censure the magazine, which would in effect put it out of business. After some negotiations, Acton and Simpson passed the whole property over to Newman, in order to save it – Newman reluctantly and with foreboding (it was 'like a bad dream') taking on the responsibility, and at Bishop Ullathorne's wish, because he felt the periodical should continue.

Newman's editorship of the *Rambler* was excellent, and very short-lived. The March issue, which he brought out, was criticised by *The Tablet*, which was back in London now and in the hands of people close to Wiseman. In the following number for May, out of loyalty to Acton and Simpson, Newman defended their right to speak out, and said that bishops must 'really desire to know the opinion of the laity on subjects in which the laity are especially concerned'. Then Bishop Ullathorne called on Newman to say he agreed with *The Tablet's* criticism, and to gently remonstrate with him over his editorial policy. In his own memorandum afterwards, Newman quoted Ullathorne as saying: 'Our laity were a peaceable set; the Church was *peace*. They had a deep faith; they did not like to hear that anyone doubted ... I said in answer that he saw one side, I another; that the Bishops etc. did not see the state of the laity ... He said something like "Who are the laity?" I answered (not those *words*) that the Church would look foolish without them.' The upshot was that Ullathorne advised him to resign the magazine back to its owners, after the July issue, to which Newman agreed.

But that July 1859 number is the one for which the *Rambler* is remembered, for in it there appeared Newman's own article, 'On Consulting the Faithful in Matters of Doctrine'. In the light of all that had happened, he felt it his duty to highlight the place of the laity in the Church. Taking a large perspective on the matter, he argued that the consent of the laity had been vital to the development and transmission of the Church's teachings. He saw the laity's consent as a sort of instinct, a quality of evaluation and judgment (*phronema*), deep in the mystical body of Christ. The direction of the Holy Spirit is among the faithful, as an answer to their prayer, and leading to a jealousy of error. Historically, as he knew from his research into the *Arians of the Fourth Century*, there had even been a time when the fidelity of the faithful had ensured the Church's continuance, 'when the body of the bishops failed in their confession of the faith'. He believed, therefore, that the Church was healthiest when able to encourage people to an intelligent grasp of their faith, and weakest when only requiring of them 'a *fides implicita* in her word, which in the educated classes will terminate in indifference, and in the poorer in superstition'.[2]

This was too much for the authorities. The theologian Dr Gillow of Ushaw College, who had already been critical of Newman over his remarks in the May issue, was seriously alarmed over the July article, and wrote about it to Bishop Brown of Newport in Wales. It was discussed at the July Synod of Bishops, and afterwards Bishop Brown delated Newman for heresy to the Congregation of Propaganda in Rome, saying his views were 'totally subversive of the authority of the Church in Matters of Faith'. But Newman was told not a word. On 11 November he preached the sermon, 'The Tree Beside the Waters',[3] at the funeral of Dr Henry Weedall, President of Oscott, who had been one of the old school of gentle Catholics, and who had suffered in being put aside during the rise of Wiseman. Only then, at Oscott, did Newman hear about his delation to Rome.

In the middle of January 1860 Ullathorne, who had returned from a visit to Rome, asked to see Newman, who was in bed with a bad cold. When he heard it was about the delation, he got up immediately and went over to see him. Ullathorne said he had heard that the Pope was 'much pained' about offending passages in the article. In response, Newman agreed to write to Wiseman, then in Rome, saying he would submit to whatever clarification the authorities there required of him. This he did, and Propaganda, on receipt of his letter, passed on to Wiseman a list of the statements in the article requiring correction. But Wiseman never sent Propaganda's list back to Newman, with its request for clarification. Instead, four months later, he heard from Henry Edward Manning, Provost of Westminster, who wrote to say that Wiseman on his return would bring the matter 'to an acceptable termination'. That was all he ever heard. And meanwhile Rome, hearing nothing further from Wiseman on the subject, and receiving no reply from Newman, simply believed he had declined to take the trouble to defend himself.

The whole episode is reminiscent of *Tract 90*, when Newman had tried to claim Catholicity for the Church of England, only to be disowned for his efforts. Now he had tried to uphold the place of the laity in the Catholic Church itself, to find himself rejected once more by those above him. As for the *Rambler*, it continued for a while (Newman occasionally making contributions to it), until Acton renamed it *Home and Foreign Review*, and which in turn was also criticised by the bishops. But after the Pope's authoritarian Brief to the Congress of Catholic Scholars at Munich in December 1863, which Acton believed condemned free enquiry in scientific and historical research, he discontinued it in April 1864. The field was left open entirely to the Ultramontane publications, especially the *Dublin Review* under William George Ward, with no organ of moderate opinion available to English Catholics.

The years ahead were dark and painful for Newman, in fact the most difficult in his life. Outwardly, perhaps there was little to indicate that this was so. He went ahead with the duties that were his, managed community affairs, and carried on with his large correspondence. He could only look on helplessly at the wider picture of developments in the Church. Considered unsound, and difficult to deal with, the important people in London had ensured he was kept at a safe distance, as they were moving ahead with their own agenda of Catholic extremism. And on the opposite or liberal side there were those, including the impatient young Acton, who were becoming disappointed with him too. He had wished them to use more prudence and tact in dealings with Church authority, to leaven their ideals with a sense of what was actually possible, and to have the wisdom to see that good things often have to wait for their season of recognition and acceptance. For some of them, it seemed now that the older Newman was becoming too intellectually cautious, and was rowing back from his earlier wholehearted support for their views. They did not realise how completely his position had been undermined in the Church, and at what personal and hidden cost to himself.

Jotting down thoughts in an exercise book at this time, he did admit that he had lost his youthful natural enthusiasm. 'When I was young I was bold, because I was ignorant – now I have lost my boldness because I have advanced in experience.' And the experience of being a Catholic included many failures, and the unkindness shown him. So while he could depend on Christ's presence in the Church, nevertheless 'the separate members of the Church, my Superiors, though they may claim my obedience, have no claim on my admiration, and offer nothing for my inward trust'. He realised that 'because I have not retailed gossip, flattered great people, and sided with this or that party, I am nobody'. He renewed a lifelong prayer of his, to be 'set aside in the world', in keeping with the ideal of his patron St Philip, 'to despise being despised'. And yet he found he could not free himself from anxiety, or from that acute sense of failure and helplessness, which led him to worry both about his own health and also again about the future of the Oratory.[4]

Not surprisingly, the cumulative effect of all the blows of past years, together with his conviction that he was repeatedly made the scapegoat for others' shortcomings, had brought him almost to the point of breaking. Suffering from insomnia into the summer of 1860, and strongly advised to get away for some months' rest, Newman first took three weeks away, in the company of William Paine Neville, who had been among the group received by him from St Saviour's in Leeds, and had subsequently joined the Oratory. They went to see his childhood house at Ham, next visited Brighton, where his sister Mary was buried, and then went to spend time in Cambridge. Still he was depressed, with anxiety, as he put it, 'sucking life' out of him. Afterwards he went out to Rednal, spending the rest of the summer there. Meanwhile in August the quiet Frederick Bowles, all the time with him since Littlemore, suddenly left the Oratory. The brother of his friend Emily Bowles, Newman had often been concerned about him, since he was so withdrawn by nature and needed continual encouragement. His departure meant Newman had to take responsibility for music in the church. Later in the year, however, he managed to get away for rest on two more occasions, to Ventnor on the Isle of Wight, and then to London.

But a more pressing cause of worry was soon upon him, centred on the Oratory school, and which would result in a full-blown crisis. Although Newman had ultimate responsibility for the school, Fr Nicholas Darnell in fact, as the headmaster, and with the backing of the lay staff and influential friends, was making it independent of the Oratory and ambitiously building it up to rival the public schools. He was also, without consultation with his fellow Oratorians or with Newman, intending to move it to a better site. Newman himself was hearing criticisms from outside, including, worryingly, about severe punishments. Matters eventually came to a head in the winter of 1861–2, when Darnell demanded the immediate resignation of Mrs Wootten, the school's matron, on the grounds of her excessive mollycoddling of sick or delicate boys. The convert widow of a popular Tractarian Oxford doctor, Frances Wootten had both been loyal to Newman and a friend of Darnell in the school. Conscious of what it must be like for them to be away from home, Newman was deeply appreciative of her maternal interest in the boys, as he had wanted a quality of care that was not usually available in boarding-schools.

Confronted with this peremptory demand, and even though Mrs Wootten offered to resign, Newman could see no reason why she should do so. After attempting a compromise, he was presented after Christmas with a stark ultimatum, whereby Darnell and his teachers said they would resign if Newman failed to dismiss her. His response was to ask the community's prayers and opinion, and, finding them in general agreement with what he intended to do, he forthwith accepted the resignation of Darnell and the teachers. In the process, he discovered Frances Wootten's real crime in Darnell's eyes was 'insubordination' – she had boldly taken issue with him for not consulting Newman about the proposed transfer of the school. Immediately now he set about organising a new staff, with Ambrose St John stepping in as headmaster, and the school reopening in January only a few days late. He even got Tom Arnold to come from Dublin as senior master. Arnold, poorly paid in the University, had felt his position there was insecure, and was glad when St John travelled over to negotiate his release, and could offer a small house nearby in Birmingham for himself and his growing family. Two of Darnell's teachers apologised, and were reinstated. But Darnell himself was devastated, and departed quickly from the Oratory, despite Newman's pleading with him to take time and avoid a hasty decision.

As for Frances Wootton, Newman said to an enquiring boy's father that it 'would have been unjust, ungrateful, cowardly, disloyal to the Oratory, and utterly disgraceful', to have agreed to 'the immediate dismissal of a helpless lady, who had no kind of warning of what was coming, and who had in many ways sacrificed herself for us'.[5] And to Mrs Peter Bretherton, wife of a local Catholic employer, he added: 'Every woman's heart would have cried shame on me, if I had been the coward to banish, or permit to be banished a lady and benefactress, at a minute's warning (whatever maybe her alleged faults) at the dictation of a lot of men.'[6] As if to confirm this, many mothers wrote to him afterwards, in appreciation of the stand he took. The school itself survived and did well under St John's headship, while Newman would find himself much involved in it over the years ahead, helping in a variety of roles, including teaching, directing plays, and writing letters and reports to parents. Frances Wootten would continue to be a great strength, and be loyal to the end of her days. And Nicholas Darnell, after an intervening period of three years, had the courage to write acknowledging that he had been 'insufferably violent and headstrong and conceited' – and, although not coming back, there was a genuine reconciliation effected.

But the extreme fragility of the community was shown up later that year, when Stanislas Flanagan also departed. Unsettled since his bout of tuberculosis, Stanislas had come to believe that the Oratory was incapable of succeeding and was 'going to the dogs'. Newman, who thought the world of him, had especially valued his theological acumen and practical advice. His departure now, he said, was 'the most tragical event which has befallen the Oratory since it has been set up'. But his loss would be a great gain elsewhere. Working on in Smethwick for a few years, Stanlislas then returned to Ireland, where, through the good offices of Edwin Wyndham Quin, Lord Dunraven, he became the revered and long-lived parish priest of Adare in County Limerick. It meant he was close to the homes of Dunraven in Adare, Aubrey de Vere in Curraghchase, and William Monsell in Tervoe, all converts through Newman, and in different ways influential in the Ireland of their time. Stanislas would also remain on warm terms with the Oratorians back in Birmingham.

Despite the endless practical matters occupying him, and although frustrated at the lack of use of his intellectual talents, Newman's mind was still from time to time turning over the great issues he felt were crying out to be addressed. Looking in particular at the spectre of growing unbelief around him, he felt a need to confront the phenomenon – and to offer to his contemporaries, if he could, a rationale for the great reasonableness of faith. It was the subject approached already in his Oxford *University Sermons*, but now needing further elucidation. All around were the signs of the disintegration of religious belief, with a drifting away from the moorings of institutionalised Christianity. He thought that fundamental Protestantism had little by way of an answer, its simplistic Bible faith threatened by the implications of Darwin's *Origin of Species*, published in 1859. Anglicanism in general still seemed in the eyes of many to offer only a feeble antidote, and the Catholic Church itself, while having latent but powerful resources at its disposal, just then officially was closing its mind to the pressing challenges of the age.

The phenomenon of unbelief was not an abstract one for Newman. He had seen his own brothers discard the faith handed onto them, Charles very quickly embracing an atheistic socialist philosophy, and Frank more slowly travelling from disillusionment with Evangelicalism, through Unitarianism and into becoming a free-thinker. He was also in correspondence on matters of faith with his longstanding friend, the railway and naval engineer William Froude – who could not himself find the way to religious belief, though his wife Catherine and their children became Catholics under Newman's tutelage. Many noted figures in that Victorian era were likewise in a quandary over issues of faith and reason, or becoming 'agnostic', to use the word soon to be coined by T.H. Huxley. For instance the novelist George Eliot, one of the greatest of Newman's contemporaries, had found her fervent Evangelical faith gradually shipwrecked (just at the time when he was turning to Rome), mainly through the influence of German Higher Criticism, and as she was translating the noted but corrosive *Das Leben Jesu* by David Friederich Strauss. All of this, indeed, had already formed the background to Newman's fight against Liberalism in Oxford, when with Keble and Pusey he had sought to counteract the rationalistic influences undermining the gift of faith in people's hearts.

At various times over these years, Newman made out notes for himself, trying to find ways of outlining the rational foundations for faith. Not a professional philosopher himself, he found that entering into its various schools 'is to my own feelings like entering into a labyrinth'.[7] But he kept searching and analysing, relying in the end on his own resources, and hoping that eventually he would produce something worthwhile, to counter the widespread scepticism, and to argue against the notion that modern progress in knowledge inevitably led to the discarding of religious belief. He wanted to show that the faith of even children and unlearned persons was deeply reasonable, not requiring 'books or education, or an array of facts'.[8] It would be some years yet before he would work out and then publish his approach, in the *Grammar of Assent*.

More than this, however, was his unwavering belief that the Catholic Church was the great historical carrier and proclaimer of Christian faith, and the providential bulwark against the forces of unbelief. This he held absolutely, despite his bitter experience of the injustice of some of its ministers, and his knowledge of its history of sin and serious failure. He would often say that there was really no middle ground between Catholicism and unbelief, and that the proper fulfilment of any form of Christian faith was its Catholic realisation, as otherwise there was little to halt the slide away from faith. A battle was going on, therefore, between faith and unbelief – Newman viewing this struggle, all the time since his early Oxford days, in dramatic and biblical apocalyptic terms. He feared greatly the spectre of a growing atheism in the future, and what might be its dreadful consequences. In an often-quoted letter to an Anglican correspondent at this time he wrote:

> My own belief is, that, if there be a God, Catholicism is true; but this is the elementary, august, and sovereign truth, the denial of which is in progress. May He Himself give grace to those who shall be alive in that terrible day, to fight His battle well. All the forms of Protestantism, allow me to say, are but toys of children in the great battle between the Holy Catholic Roman Church and Antichrist.[9]

His own withdrawal from public view, however, gave rise to much speculation, including word going round that physically and mentally he was breaking up. At one point he issued a sharp public rebuff to persistent talk in Protestant circles that he now deeply regretted his move to Rome, by contrasting the undoubted consolation he found in ordinary Catholic life and liturgy with his often dreary experience of Anglican worship. Perhaps that was hurtful to some, but he felt he had to make his own position absolutely clear.

The first photographs taken of him date from this period. They show him already with heavily lined features, and hair going white. One of the few people who came to know about the real reasons for his silence was Emily Bowles. On a visit to him in 1861 she was shocked by his aged appearance, and the sense of terrible weariness in him, even though she would never forget the brightness of his welcome. Two years later he poured out his heart to her in two long letters, letting her in on how he was subjected to suspicions, and had to act with extreme care or else fall victim to the Congregation of Propaganda in Rome, which still had charge of England as a missionary country. He told her it was 'a quasi-military power, extraordinary, for missionary countries, rough and ready'. He feared a call to Rome, as had been rumoured at one point, and he named a few people who had been summoned there by the Congregation, to wait on it and having to account for themselves, only to be broken by the experience. And, while he was willing to observe St Philip's rule that 'we should despise being despised', he felt rightly impatient at the scorn and contempt which was injuring his Oratory.[10]

Again, he was made to take more decent holidays over these summers, at Deal and Ramsgate, where he read novels including *Bleak House* by Dickens, and then on the continent – his first there since travelling with the Froudes thirty years before, and now visiting Paris, Treves, the Moselle, the Rhine, Aix-la-Chapelle and Ostend. It was while he was setting off on this latter holiday, in July 1863, that he called to see Faber in London, who after many false alarms was finally dying, and had asked to see him. At their short meeting, Faber spoke most of the time, Newman feeling he wanted to disburden his mind, while still trying to maintain that he had never been disloyal despite the quarrel between the Oratories. He protested his love and admiration, after which Newman blessed him, and then departed. Faber rallied then, but died later on 26 September, and Newman and St John went up to London for the funeral.

Yet quite a wonderful turnaround began for him now, towards the end of these hidden years. Slowly and almost imperceptibly, some of his dearest friends of Oxford days, who had remained as Anglicans, were in the process of renewing their contact with him. Of his former curates, only the ever-faithful J.R. Bloxam had continued in correspondence. But now two of the others, Isaac Williams and William Copeland, were in communication again. Copeland had run into him on a London street, and then acceded to Newman's repeated entreaties to pay him a visit in Birmingham. And, returning from his continental holiday, he found awaiting him a letter from John Keble, the first in seventeen years, expressing sorrow for not having written, and having heard that the silence of old friends had pained him. Newman wrote back straightaway: 'Never have I doubted for one moment your affection for me – never have I been hurt at your silence … You are always with me a thought of reverence and love – and there is nothing I love better than you, and Isaac, and Copeland, and many others I could name, except Him whom I ought to love best of all and supremely.'[11]

Then on 30 August, as he was arranging books in the library, he was called down to the door, to find Frederic Rogers there, who had cut off from him twenty years before. Now aged fifty-two, and Under-Secretary to the Colonies, Rogers burst into tears when he saw Newman, and would not let go his hands, first saying, 'How altered you are', and then crying out, 'Oh, how like *you*!' They had much to talk about, and found they had still a great deal in common: 'It was almost like two clocks keeping time', Newman reported afterwards to St John. And Rogers wrote to his wife about their meeting, saying how upset he was to see Newman almost alone in the large house, overworked, and 'thrown away by the communion to which he has devoted himself'. He sensed, rightly, that Newman's isolation among Catholics was sending him back to his old Anglican friends. It can be said that these renewed bonds from former days were among the greatest gifts to adorn the later years of Newman's life. And, despite the very real Church divide separating them, there was surely now a greater mystery of grace at work, uniting in a new way this circle of friends once sadly parted.

NOTES

1. cf. Placid Murray, *Newman the Oratorian*, pp. 351–2.
2. cf. John Coulson (ed.), *On Consulting the Faithful in Matters of Doctrine*, London: Geoffrey Chapman, 1961, pp. 20–5, 53–106.
3. *SVO*, pp. 243–62.
4. *AW*, pp. 251–3.
5. *LD*, XX, p. 117.
6. Ibid., p. 119.
7. Hugo de Achaval and J. Derek Holmes (eds), *The Theological Papers of John Henry Newman on Faith and Certainty*, Oxford: Clarendon Press, 1976, p. 52.
8. Ibid., p. 87.
9. *LD*, XIX, pp. 487–8.
10. *LD*, XX, pp. 445–8, 453–4.
11. Ibid., pp. 502–3.

— CHAPTER 9 —

Finding His Voice Again

NEWMAN'S EMERGENCE FROM obscurity took place in extraordinary circumstances. While his Anglican friends, and others like Emily Bowles especially, looked on helplessly, all he could do himself was simply keep going with the daily duties which were his lot in the Oratory. Since Stanislas had left he had taken over the accounts, and his willingness to cover for the others meant there was often much activity in the parish to engage him, as well as the school. For him, the Oratory's role within the great expanse of Birmingham and its people was very important, its small group of priests ministering over a large area, and the Oratory itself a centre where many could find sustenance and support. And, despite their occasional differences, he admired and respected his Bishop, with Ullathorne too valuing the work of the Oratorians in his diocese. But still there was the weight upon him of rejection, which both Emily Bowles and Frederic Rogers had noticed, which could almost overwhelm him sometimes, leaving him with a sense of uselessness. There was a day, for instance, when he opened again his exercise book, to write how he had awoken that morning, feeling so strongly that he was 'cumbering the ground', and almost unable to get ready to face the day. 'I said, what is the good of trying to preserve or increase strength, when nothing comes of it? What is the good of living for nothing?'[1]

And then another day came, 30 December 1863, when a friend sent him in the post a copy of *Macmillan's Magazine* for January, which, in a review of James Anthony Froude's *History of England*, contained the assertion: 'Truth, for its own sake, had never been a virtue with the Roman clergy. Father Newman informs us that it need not, and on the whole ought not to be; that cunning is the weapon which Heaven has given to the saints wherewith to withstand the brute male force of the wicked world which marries and is given in marriage'. Newman wrote at once to the publishers about the remark, and concluded: 'I do but wish to draw the attention of yourselves, as gentlemen, to a grave and gratuitous slander, with which I feel confident you will be sorry to find associated a name so eminent as yours.'

Soon Newman found out that the reviewer was none other than Charles Kingsley, the chaplain to Queen Victoria, a popular novelist, and Regius Professor of Modern History at Cambridge. Newman was amazed, as he explained to Alexander Macmillan, head of the publishing firm, because he had presumed the author was some 'young scribe, who is making a cheap reputation by smart hits at safe objects'. And all Kingsley could do, in justification for his remark, was refer to Newman's Anglican writings, especially his sermon 'Wisdom and Innocence'. But this fed on the popular belief that Newman and his fellow-Tractarians had been dishonest crypto-Catholics. There followed a correspondence, in which Kingsley was willing to say he had mistaken the meaning of Newman's words, thereby offering what seemed like an apology, but which Newman considered insincere. Newman then got Longmans to publish in pamphlet form the letters between them, entitled *Mr Kingsley and Dr Newman – A Correspondence*, and containing his own sharp satirical observations on Kingsley's equivocation. A best seller, it provoked Kingsley to respond with a pamphlet of his own, *What, then, does Dr Newman Mean?* There, with unrestrained language, he set out what he saw as the efforts of superstitious Catholicism to undermine the English Protestant ideal of Christian manliness, a prime example of which could be seen in the craft and subtlety used by his priest opponent.

While some might have adjudged that there was right and wrong on both sides, many observers could see that Kingsley's rough continuing attack on Newman was unfair in itself. Matters might have remained there – except that Newman, who always admitted he needed an 'external stimulous' to go into action, now became clear about what he needed to do. In effect, as Newman wrote to Copeland, since Kingsley's argument appealed to the continuing prejudice '*that I was a Papist while I was an Anglican* … The only way in which I can destroy this, is to give my history, and the history of my mind, from 1822 or earlier, down to 1845'. He would therefore have to write an *Apologia*, an exposition and defence of the growth of his religious views. In doing this, he would importantly rebut the accusation, now twenty years old, of Romanist dishonesty among the Tractarians, while also hoping to prove the Catholic Church's inherent love of truth, in spite of the flaws within it, of which he was so well aware. In prospect, it was a huge undertaking, and one which he must do at once, while interest was aroused in so many, if he was to disarm the still widespread prejudices supporting Kingsley's tirade.

He decided to bring out his account from Longmans in weekly pamphlets, with the first part appearing on Thursday, 21 April 1864, followed by six more parts on the consecutive Thursdays, and an appendix published two weeks later, on 16 June. The first part was his answer to Kingsley's method, which in essence, he said, was an attempt to cut the ground from under his feet, and 'poison by anticipation the public mind against me, John Henry Newman, and to infuse into the imaginations of my readers, suspicion and mistrust of every thing that I may say in reply to him. This I call *poisoning the wells*'.[2] The main chapters then told from week to week the story of his own developing religious views, up to 1845, and concluded with a defence of the Catholic Church as 'the oracle of God' in the midst of history. There followed in the appendix a series of notes and supplementary material.

His work-rate for this time was astonishing, often up to sixteen hours a day and once twenty-two hours spent standing at his upright desk, as he drafted and rewrote the chapters. Throughout, he was consulting by correspondence with his confreres of the Oxford years, all in order to tell the truth about that time, and then 'leave the matter in God's hands', as he said to Keble. And everywhere the brown-covered pamphlets were being read, and the next Thursday's instalment eagerly awaited, by all kinds of people, including members of a younger generation, among whom were the future literary figures Gerard Manley Hopkins and Thomas Hardy.

This was how Newman's famous *Apologia pro Vita Sua*, as the work was entitled when published in a single volume soon after, came to be born. The 'Defence of his Life', it is one of the great stories in the long history of religious literature. While rooted in the very particular events of the growth of the Oxford Movement, the work is full of keen feeling and honesty, the central chapters taking readers into the sweep of the author's vision, his relationship with many gifted individuals, and into the depth of his own religious faith, as it evolved over the years since his Evangelical conversion in 1816, through 1833, and up to 1845. In the chapter subsequent to these, 'Position of my Mind since 1845', he sets out memorably his belief in 'the being of a God', which is as certain to him as his own personal existence – although he looks out with distress on the vast world, so full of alienation and conflict, 'which seems to give the lie to that great truth, of which my being is so full'. He sees God's intervening in humanity's bewildering contradictory history as leading to the establishment of Christ's Catholic Church, to purify and restore through grace, and to teach with infallible authority. Yet his understanding of the exercise of that authority is careful, acknowledging the instances of its abuse, while showing the ways in which aspects of the truth have been clarified over the Christian ages.[3] As for the Anglican Church, in a supplementary note he writes of seeing it now as 'a mere national institution', and yet truly as 'the instrument of Providence in conferring great benefits on me'. He would wish to avoid anything 'which went to weaken its hold upon the public mind, or to unsettle its establishment, or to embarrass and lessen its maintenance of those great Christian and Catholic principles and doctrines which it has up to this time successfully preached'.[4]

At the conclusion of the chapter, 'Position of my Mind since 1845', there is a moving tribute to his small community in the Oratory,

Ambrose St John, Austin Mills, Henry Bittleston, Edward Caswall, William Neville and Ignatius Ryder. Often considered of little account in the world at large, these people were his family, 'with whom I have lived so long, with whom I hope to die'. In addition, he remembered all those of former Oxford years who had been his 'thorough friends', some of whom had become Catholics while others had remained Anglicans. Many of these indeed had helped him unstintingly during the composition of the *Apologia*, including Pusey, who had hardly ever lost contact with him, and also now Richard Church, renewing a friendship broken for twenty years. Newman ended by praying 'for this whole company, with a hope against hope, that all of us, who once were so united, and so happy in our union, may even now be brought at length, by the Power of the Divine Will, into One Fold and under One Shepherd'.[5]

The *Apologia* was a phenomenon, taking the country by storm, and led to Newman's name having a greater influence than it had at the height of the Oxford Movement, a quarter of a century earlier. He became respected now both at home and overseas, and by so many who still did not share his beliefs, but who looked to him as a person of integrity and of great mind. One of those who read the *Apologia* at this time was George Eliot, who was without conscious faith for twenty years now. She wrote to a friend saying she was indignant at Kingsley's 'arrogance, coarse impertinence and unscrupulousness', but was moved by Newman's work as 'the revelation of a life – how different in form from one's own, yet with how close a fellowship in its needs and burthens – I mean spiritual needs and burthens'.[6] Some of the most positive responses came from Nonconformist sources, as well as from Anglicans. And Catholic diocesan priests were especially appreciative of his writing in their defence: their honesty, their 'self-devotion' and 'discipline' standing out for him, as he said in the *Apologia*, from his very first days as a Catholic.

But the Catholic authorities in London were less than enamoured with his success, as became clear later that year, when Newman was offered for sale a plot of land in Oxford. Previously, when there were tentative moves to build a church or have a Catholic presence in Oxford (which was within the Birmingham diocese), Newman had not been in favour, feeling anything of that nature might destabilise the still important Anglican work done in the university. Now he was more open to some Catholic presence, and especially as Ullathorne went further and asked him to take charge of a mission in Oxford. Still, Newman was hesitant, and torn, especially as Pusey thought such a move might only cause controversy, although Newman tried to assure him that perhaps only an Oratory would be set up, and solely to cater for the spiritual needs of Catholic students. However he soon realised that the bishops in general, and Rome, were against anything which might attract Catholics to Oxford. Ullathorne in consequence withdrew his support. The plot of land had to be given up, therefore, and with the help of Pusey was sold to the university.

The person most in opposition to the Oxford proposal, and especially to Newman's going there, was the formidable Henry Edward Manning. Holding strong Ultramontane views, he had become Provost of Westminster, and advisor to Wiseman. In addition, he was exercising much influence in Rome through the Papal Chamberlain, Monsignor George Talbot. Born in 1808, Manning had considered a political career before taking orders in the Church of England, and was a close friend of William Gladstone. He had four years of happy marriage before his wife, Caroline Sargent, took ill and died. A zealous pastor, he continued with the strength of his faith, and was particularly interested in social problems, both as curate of Lavington and later when Archdeacon of Chichester. In April 1851, after the Gorham Judgment, he converted to Catholicism, was ordained priest by Wiseman just two months later, and sent to the Accademia die Nobili Ecclesiastici in Rome, 'the nursery of Cardinals'. Having expressed the wish to remain by Wiseman's side, and having gained his complete confidence, Manning was clearly from the first destined for high office in the Catholic Church.

He especially had been alarmed at the prospect of Newman going to Oxford, and was the one who had taken steps to alert Rome and get the move stopped. Both as an Anglican and as a Catholic Manning had initially favoured Newman, but more recently had grown to suspect the orthodoxy of his views. As an Ultramontane, for instance, he strongly supported the Temporal Power of the Pope, which was under threat at this time; Newman by contrast felt the subject was open to question. Manning was also less than pleased with Newman's role in the *Rambler* affair, and with his championing the place of the laity. And when the *Apologia* came out, he had little sympathy for it, being of one mind with his younger disciple, Herbert Vaughan (later to succeed· him as Cardinal Archbishop of Westminster), who wrote: 'I have read it with a mixture of pain and pleasure. The egotism may be disgusting, but it is venial. There are views put forward which I abhor, and which fill me with pain and suspicion.'

Manning's principal contact in Rome was Monsignor George Talbot, a Papal Chamberlain – who had daily contact with the Pope, and was considered to be his most confidential friend and favourite. The younger son of Lord Talbot of Malahide in County Dublin, he had been received into the Church in 1843 by Wiseman, who was responsible for placing him by the Pope's side. Unfriendly to Newman from some time back, he was close to Manning and Vaughan, and would be especially in the conflicts which lay ahead. Newman certainly had done himself no service when Talbot, sensing the general change of opinion in Newman's favour after the *Apologia*, tried to flatter by inviting him to Rome to preach to 'an audience of Protestants more educated than could ever be the case in England', to which he received the curt reply: 'However, Birmingham people have souls; and I have neither taste nor talent for the sort of work which you cut out for me. And I beg to decline your offer'.

On 15 February 1865 Cardinal Wiseman died, having been in poor health for some years, and often away from London. At his funeral, people in their thousands turned out to watch the procession, it being said that never since the state funeral of the Duke of Wellington had London witnessed such a sight. It showed the measure of Wiseman's achievement, and the rise in esteem for the Catholic Church, over the nearly fifteen years since the Catholic hierarchy had been restored in such unpromising circumstances. And now, although not on the Chapter's list sent to Rome, his successor turned out to be Manning, who with the urging of Talbot was very much the Pope's personal choice. A Catholic for just fourteen years, it was a huge personal honour for him. It was also a triumph for the authoritarian Ultramontane view, with its chief lay spokesman, the former fiery Tractarian William George Ward, now editor of the *Dublin Review*, exulting in his appointment. Looking noticeably pale and intense, Manning was consecrated by Ullathorne at St Mary Moorfields, the Westminster Pro-Cathedral, on 6 June following, with Newman attending among the secular clergy. He was not present at the banquet afterwards, a fact that did not go down well with Manning (or in Rome). In addition, having heard beforehand that Manning wished to make him an honorary bishop, Newman had made it clear he would not accept, suspecting that it would be a move to 'muzzle' him.

The scene was being set for the last series of challenges and conflicts which would fill Newman's life. It would have a large canvas. Abroad, with the diminished Papal States under serious threat from the expanding Kingdom of Italy, the Pope in defiance had just issued his expected condemnation of 'the principal errors of our times', in the Syllabus of Errors, accompanying the encyclical *Quanta Cura*, in late 1864. Among the eighty propositions condemned was: 'The Roman Pontiff can and should reconcile and harmonise himself with progress, with liberalism, and with recent civilisation.' But although 'progress, liberalism and recent civilisation' in an Italian context implied violent secularist attacks on the Church and its institutions, in some of the wider world of Europe and North America, where the terms had a generally positive meaning, Catholic hierarchies were embarrassed and the ordinary faithful nonplussed. Other propositions condemned included support for religious toleration and freedom of speech, although again these terms had special reference to the situation in Italy and elsewhere in Europe.

Newman was not unduly disturbed by the Syllabus, and could, like the liberal Bishop Dupanloup in France, offer a context and 'minimalist' interpretation of the document. He admitted finding its tone 'alarming', but held out the sanguine hope that, sooner or later, there was bound to be a reaction and a greater balance reached. In the meantime, with Manning as the new Archbishop, with Ward running the *Dublin Review*, and Talbot in Rome, he had little confidence in the immediate direction the Church would take in

England. While he was fond of Ward, because always he knew where he stood with him, he found he could not trust Manning – 'he is so mysterious, that I don't know how one can ever have confidence in him' – although he momentarily hoped that he might take a more 'moderate line', now that he was 'at the top of the tree'.

His contacts with old Anglican friends brought both sadness and joy. At the beginning of May Isaac Williams died, Newman having visited him less than a week before – the first visit in twenty-two years, and the last. Before that, during his days in London for Manning's consecration, Newman had stayed with Frederic Rogers, and met Richard Church for the first time since 1846. His two friends that summer sent him three violins, from which to choose one as a gift. Only a few months before he had taken out his old violin, 'after sixteen years of utter and absolute separation from it', as he told Jemima. Now he had a better one, chosen after 'having a good bout at Beethoven's Quartets', and which made him 'cry out with delight'.

Early that year he himself had been indulging in a composition of his own, but a literary one, finding on 17 January a sudden inspiration, and writing down what became known as *The Dream of Gerontius* 'till it was finished, on small bits of paper'. Wanting to support a new magazine, *The Month*, founded the year before by Fanny Margaret Taylor and now being handed over by her to the Jesuits, Newman had *The Dream of Gerontius* published there in two parts, in the issues for May and June 1865. His longest poetic work, it describes the journey of the soul of Gerontius from this life to Purgatory, lovingly eager to behold the face of God. It is remembered above all for the hymn, 'Praise to the Holiest in the Height'. Later, of course, it was to become immortalised when put to music in Edward Elgar's oratorio, one of the best-loved choral works of modern times. In it, more than anywhere else, people of divergent beliefs are often drawn together in their listening – into Newman's Catholic consciousness and vision, where the world beyond, in all its mystery, enters so personally into our own.

On 12 September there occurred a meeting between Newman, Keble and Pusey, at Keble's vicarage in Hursley. There had been hopes of an earlier one between Keble and Newman, but postponed due to

Keble's wife Charlotte being seriously ill. Now, while heading to the Isle of Wight, Newman stayed over at Southampton and decided to go up to Hursley. There he found Keble at the door of his house, and Pusey unexpectedly inside, but Keble's wife absent, having taken ill again. An extraordinary encounter, Newman described it poignantly afterwards to Ambrose St John: 'As we three sat together at one table, I had as painful thoughts as I ever recollect, though it was a pain, not acute, but heavy. There were three old men, who had worked together vigorously in their prime. This is what they have come to – poor human nature – after twenty years they meet together round a table, but without a common cause, or free outspoken thoughts – but, though kind yet subdued, and antagonistic in their mode of speaking, and all of them with broken prospects ...'[7]

They spent four hours together, and had dinner, Newman feeling at a remove from Pusey, but close to Keble: '... he is as delightful as ever – and, it *seemed* to me as if he felt a sympathy and intimacy with me which he did not find with Pusey.' Then they had to separate. Later Newman wrote: 'Just before my time for going, Pusey went to read the Evening Service in Church, and I was left in the open air with Keble by himself ... We walked a little way, and stood looking in silence at the Church and Churchyard, so beautiful and calm. Then he began to converse with me in more than his old tone of intimacy, as if we had never been parted, and soon I was obliged to go.'[8]

Afterwards, Pusey had a letter published in the Anglo-Catholic *Guardian* newspaper, to rebut a report it had carried about the meeting: 'The statement is, that Dr Newman and myself were "*reconciled* after twenty years". The deep love between us, which now dates back for above forty years, has never been in the least overshadowed. His leaving us was one of the deep sorrows of my life; but it involved separation of place, not diminution of affection.'[9]

And soon Newman was involved in a respectful controversy with him, when Pusey published a book, which was entitled *The Church of England a Portion of Christ's One Holy Catholic Church, and a Means of Restoring Visible Unity. An Eirenicon.* It hardly lived up to its peacemaking title, as an *Eirenicon*, as it attacked the more extravagant opinions, as if they were the mainstream ones, of Roman Catholics on devotion to Mary and on the Pope's infallibility. Not wishing to leave the field open just to extreme replies from Ward and Manning, Newman began working out a response which, named his *Letter to Dr Pusey*, came out at the end of January 1866. Courteous in expression, it especially set out what he considered the true and patristic Catholic doctrine on Mary. In relation to Ward and the late Fr Faber, whose views had been attacked by Pusey, Newman managed to compliment them while yet saying that 'they are in no sense spokesmen for English Catholics'. He charged Pusey with giving undue prominence to exaggerated and Italian Marian devotions, which had no place in such as the Missal, or the Roman Catechism, or the *Imitation of Christ*, or in Challoner or Wiseman.[10] The *Letter to Dr Pusey* was much appreciated by many Catholics, and by bishops including Ullathorne, the courageous and independent Dr Clifford of Clifton diocese, and even Dr Brown, who had delated Newman to Rome. But behind the scenes the Ultramontanes were angry, with Talbot saying of Newman that 'his spirit must be crushed', and Archbishop Manning in agreement, believing he had brought an alien tone of 'worldly Catholicism' into the Church, which 'will deceive many'.

Soon Newman heard the news that Keble, whom he had hoped to see again, was ill himself and not expected to live. Always for him a part of his own soul, John Keble died on Holy Thursday 1866. His wife had been expected to go before him, but lingered on for a few more weeks. Afterwards, Newman remarked how close he felt Keble was to the Catholic Church at their last meeting, even if not a visible member of it. He accepted that, unless Keble had seen his own way clearly to entering into full communion, 'he was bound to remain as he was. And it was in this way that he always put it'.[11] This he said in a letter to Fr Henry Coleridge, Jesuit editor of *The Month*, who wrote a sensitive obituary article on Keble, which Newman much appreciated.

Henry Coleridge, great-nephew of the poet Samuel Taylor Coleridge, and convert son of the judge at the Achilli trial many years before, would become a good friend of Newman. 'You, Jesuits, live fast', Newman said to him at this time, concerned that he was unwell, and had to get away after a heavy Lent's labours and Holy Week at Farm Street Church in London. Coleridge often turned to Newman for advice in the years ahead, Newman quietly encouraging him against what he felt was the ultra-caution of some of his Jesuit confreres, and wishing to help *The Month* achieve a balance absent in the *The Tablet* and in Ward's *Dublin Review*. Another contact just now was the serious young Oxford poet Gerard Manley Hopkins, who came looking for guidance, only to be surprised at Newman's laughing, easy ways and slangy speech. Hopkins was received into the Church by Newman in October 1866, and, after teaching in the Oratory School for a time, with Newman's warm encouragement entered the Jesuits in 1868.

And once again, the prospect of going to Oxford came before Newman, but initially aroused in him mixed feelings. Ullathorne had called on Palm Sunday 1866 and asked him again to undertake a mission there, on a piece of land still held by Newman, and where perhaps an Oratory chapel could be built. Not wanting a repeat of the earlier episode, Newman impressed on his Bishop the need for a clear mandate from Propaganda in Rome before he could proceed. It was Christmas before he received word from Ullathorne that Cardinal Barnabò had given his permission – leaving him now with a feeling of excitement at the prospect of starting a new and important work, especially since he believed Ullathorne was fully behind the project. His only worry was about Manning, as he frankly told Ullathorne, who he felt could undermine what they were about. But he went ahead, raising the funds necessary for a small church, and which he hoped to have under construction in the summer of 1867.

Officially, Catholics were still banned from going to Oxford, although some had gone through special dispensation. All at once Rome reiterated that ban, with Cardinal Barnabò writing to both Newman and Ullathorne about it, the letter to Newman accusing the Oratory school of preparing youths for Oxford in contravention of the ban. It was becoming evident that the permission from Rome was not as unreserved as Newman had thought it to be, and Ullathorne informed him that Talbot, Manning and others were vehemently opposed to a mission there. But unfortunately Ullathorne had kept back from Newman a 'secret instruction' in the original letter from Barnabò, which had directed Ullathorne 'blandly and softly' ('blande suaviterque') to dissuade Newman himself from any residence in Oxford, as his presence would encourage Catholics to send their sons. When an anonymous letter appeared in Henry Wilberforce's *Weekly Register* saying the Pope had forbidden Newman to go to Oxford, on account of suspicions about his orthodoxy, Ullathorne had to let Newman know about the instruction. For Newman, it looked like the end of the Oxford matter, and although he was angry with Ullathorne for withholding the instruction from him, he conceded that his Bishop was in an impossible position, caught on all sides, and a victim too of the 'double-dealing' in Rome. He was sorry that young men were still being prohibited from Oxford, because of the perceived threat to their faith: '... *all places* are dangerous, – the world is dangerous', he told a father of boys in his school. 'I do not believe that Oxford is more dangerous than Woolwich, than the army, than London. – and I think you cannot keep young men under glass cases.'[12]

Because of Barnabò's accusation about the Oratory school, Ambrose St John and Henry Bittleston had gone to Rome to clear its name, to discover that the Cardinal had a list of complaints against Newman, although not knowing that these had been fuelled not only by Talbot and Manning, but also by Herbert Vaughan who was then staying in Rome. But at least they managed to clear up the *Rambler* affair, when they discovered the charges made against Newman, which Wiseman had never made known to him. Newman, contacted by them, posted on the draft of his letter to Wiseman, where he had asked for the opportunity to explain himself, and which was never replied to. He got Ullathorne to write as well. Barnabò expressed amazement, and began to speak in very friendly terms about Newman, even saying he was a saint. The Pope himself was genuinely pleased, warmly assuring St John and Bittleston of his own regard for Newman, although telling them he would not agree to Catholics going to Protestant Oxford colleges.

That August Manning wrote to Newman, looking for a personal meeting where they could clear up any misunderstandings. Newman, although he knew he was appearing to put himself in the wrong, refused to meet him, such was his mistrust. 'It is only as time goes on, that new deeds can reverse the old,' he told him. 'There is no short cut to a restoration of confidence, when confidence has been seriously damaged.' He also formally resigned the Oxford mission that month, knowing that a Roman Rescript was about to be issued, condemning the sending of Catholics to Oxford.

Monsignor Nardi, a high Vatican official, called that month too, obviously intending to smooth things over. Newman wrote a memorandum afterwards recounting Nardi's exhortation to him: 'I was a great man – no denying it – a great writer – good style – good strong logic … I ought to be a bishop, archbishop – yes, yes – I ought, I ought – yes, a very good bishop – it *is* your line, it *is*, it *is* – it was no good my saying it was not. I ought to take the part of the Pope. "We have very few friends," he said – "*very* few" – he spoke in a very grave earnest mournful tone.' Soon he departed – 'He wanted my photograph. I gave him two'.[13] More real was a hard, ungracious letter arriving from Cardinal Barnabò soon after, warning him his school was still on trial and not approved, because boys from it might be encouraged to go to Oxford. Newman was afraid they might close the school, which had proved very successful and had made a name for itself.

Still, he was in much better spirits, compared to the years gone by. It was all down to the *Apologia*, and the appeal it made to a great range of people. In his private exercise book, he admitted he was well past the time when he would have tried to approve himself to such as Cardinal Barnabò. In one sense, therefore, 'the iron has entered into my soul. I mean that confidence in any superiors whatever never can blossom in me again. I never shall feel easy with them … God forbid that I should liken them to the "Scribes and Pharisees" – but still I obey them, as Scribes and Pharisees were to be obeyed, as God's representatives, not from devotion to *them*.' But he had inward peace, and felt he was never in such simply happy circumstances, including his being 'surrounded with dear friends … What can I want but greater gratitude and love towards the Giver of all these good things?'[14]

And he was drawing closer to some of his own family. For among the many new visitors making their way to him were his nephews, keen to meet their famous uncle. He had not been able to see them as they were growing up. Their sister Janie came too with her mother Jemima, staying to lunch, and Jemima accompanying him on the piano as they played Beethoven sonatas, in Frances Wootten's house. Then even Jemima's husband John came with her on another occasion, and Newman would go and stay with them at Derby in June 1871, after an interval of twenty-three years. But there had been another loss too, when in May 1868 Margaret Hallahan died, mourned by her Dominican community at Stone. Her life had been a remarkable one, with Newman being one of the relatively few who understood her, she believed. In turn, her regard for him had been 'something special', as Sister Imelda Poole said to Newman afterwards.

On the wider front, despite the opposition of Manning and others, Newman was aware he had the support of great numbers of both clergy and laity up and down the country. One instance of that support was the Address presented to him back in April 1867, signed by nearly two hundred names from among the most prominent Catholic laity, headed by Lord Edward Howard, the deputy Earl Marshall, and organised at the Stafford Club (the Catholic laymen's club in London) by the devoted William Monsell. Indignant at the anonymous letter in the *Weekly Register* impugning his orthodoxy, and at the 'secret instruction' from Propaganda, the Address stated that 'every blow that touches you inflicts a wound upon the Catholic Church in this country. We hope, therefore, that you will not think it presumptuous in us to express our gratitude for all we owe you, and to assure you how heartily we appreciate the services which, under God, you have been the means of rendering our holy religion.'

The Address caused a flurry of letters between Manning in Westminster and Talbot in Rome, with the Archbishop saying it was 'a revelation of the absence of Catholic instinct, and the presence of a spirit dangerous in many'. Talbot replied that the laity 'are beginning to show the cloven foot ... They are only putting into practice the doctrine taught by Dr Newman in his article in the *Rambler*'. And he added, 'What is the province of the laity? To hunt, to shoot, to entertain. These matters they understand, but to meddle with ecclesiastical matters they have no right at all … Dr Newman is the most dangerous man in England, and you will see that he will make use of the laity against your Grace.'

Newman would not have been too alarmed, had he known what was being said about him. He was at a remove now from such attitudes among the ecclesiastical authorities. He felt instead he was 'as covered with blessings and as full of God's gifts, as is conceivable', and was aware especially of having so many well-wishers and friends, including in the Protestant world, but among the great mass of Catholics also. Yet he wondered, 'Then comes the question, what use can I make of these fresh mercies? Not from any supernatural principle, but from mere natural temper, I keep saying, What is the good of all this? What comes of it? Vanitas vanitatum, if it is but empty praise. What use can I make of it? For what is it given me?'[15] Perhaps the best course was to 'let well alone'. But he felt God had some purpose for him in all that had happened, including in his being calumniated. Certainly, he knew he had a voice now – and, as matters turned out, he would indeed use it well in the time ahead.

———

NOTES

1. *AW*, p. 254.
2. *Apo*, p. 81 (original edition only).
3. Ibid., pp. 238–69.
4. Ibid., pp. 339–42.
5. Ibid., pp. 283–4.
6. cf. Rosemary Ashton, *George Eliot – A Life*, London: Penguin, 1998, p. 276.
7. *LD*, XXII, p. 58.
8. *LD*, XXIV, p. 143.
9. Henry Parry Liddon, *Life of Edward Bouverie Pusey*, IV, London: Longmans, Green and Co., 1897, p. 112.
10. cf. *VM*, II, pp. 1–170.
11. *LD*, XXII, p. 209.

12. *LD*, XXIII, p. 101.
13. Ibid., pp. 318–9.
14. *AW*, pp. 262–3.
15. Ibid., pp. 263–4.

— CHAPTER 10 —

Upholding Religious Faith

IN THE LATER 1860s, there was much interest in the forthcoming Vatican General Council, which had been announced by the Pope in June 1867. Like others, Newman was looking forward to the event, the first since the Council of Trent, and which he felt was the best way for the Church to come together, look at pressing matters, and adjudicate on them. Although, as Ullathorne informed him, the Pope would have liked him to be a theological consultor during the Council's proceedings, Newman felt he would be of no help there. He had never considered himself a professional theologian. In his reply to Ullathorne, he remarked that he was hardly ever at home with ecclesiastical superiors, and never had succeeded with boards or committees: 'I always have felt out of place, and my words unreal.'

Soon however there were storm clouds gathering, when it became clear that Manning and Ward at home, in concert with Ultramontanes in France and in Italy, were pressing for the Council to be the occasion for a definition of Papal infallibility, which would apply to virtually all Papal pronouncements. For Newman, who considered an ecumenical council the proper and usual setting for the exercise of Papal infallibility, the prospect was troubling. In any case, he could not see the need for such a definition. There was no heresy to be resisted, and a definition would encourage the Pope to act alone without the bishops. At one point Manning, Ward and Talbot issued a manifesto calling for the definition, and opening with the words, 'We the people of England …', as if they represented what all true Catholics desired. For so many others, this was not the case, and Newman wrote to Ward, saying that by 'exalting your opinions into dogmas', he was making other Catholics who disagreed with him into 'a different religion to yours. I protest then … not against your tenets, but your schismatical spirit'. And the extreme Ultramontane cause was further strengthened in 1868, when Herbert Vaughan took over as editor of *The Tablet*.

But personally pleasing for Newman was the republication of his Anglican sermons at this time, under the editorship of William Copeland. Years back, he had brought out one volume of them, rewritten in a more obvious 'Catholic' vein, but it was not well received. Now however the reissued original sermons were much sought after, and appreciated by Catholics, Anglicans and Nonconformists alike. The standard eight-volume *Parochial and Plain Sermons* dates from this time, made up of his six books of *Parochial Sermons* as volumes I-VI, and the Plain Sermons book made into two, and issued as volumes VII and VIII. In early 1868 he published his *Verses on Various Occasions*, bringing together his Anglican and Catholic poetry, including *The Dream of Gerontius*. Also in 1868 his *Sermons on Subjects of the Day* was brought out again. He was happy that so many across the Christian spectrum could look to him for inspiration, and felt that they all had common cause against the great contemporary challenge of infidelity.

One day, he fulfilled a personal wish, that he should see Littlemore again. On 6 June 1868 he and Ambrose St John took the seven o'clock morning train for Abingdon, and made their way over to Littlemore. They spent five hours there, on a very hot day, his first visit in over twenty-two years. Many of his former parishioners recognised him, and were delighted. Martha King, whom he had once prepared for confirmation, hurried down to see him sitting in the garden of squire Charles Crawley and his wife, whose cottage and grounds were on land he sold them. Martha felt she could not let go of his hand. There was still, as was told him, great affection for his mother and sisters. He wept when he visited the church and saw again the memorial plaque to his mother. But he was pleased to see how Littlemore had become '*green*', from the trees planted in his time, and later by the Crawleys. In the afternoon they departed, from the small railway station now there, and were back in Birmingham by seven o'clock that evening.

Amid his other duties, Newman was devoting all the time he could to his projected book on the reasonableness of religious belief. Over the years since 1853, he had been making notes for himself, trying to outline different approaches to the problem, in order to take up once more what had been addressed in his *University Sermons* on faith and reason in the 1830s. The growing scepticism in life continually concerned him, as we have seen. Both English and European philosophies, he considered, were themselves vehicles tending towards scepticism, having no confidence in the mind's ability to reach towards reality, to have certitude in knowing, or to accept a rational basis for faith. For Newman, such philosophies were simply *unreal*, not in accord with the actual processes of our minds. He believed we legitimately desired to know, and are not satisfied with only surmising or with dry logical deductions. We are so constituted that we wish to actually comprehend and understand what really *is*, what really exists. We are therefore happy, on the basis of our intellectual enquiries, to assent to a whole range of truths. In daily life, we work on those assumptions – which Newman considered were more real than the theories of modern philosophy, which denied our certain knowing, leaving us only in a subjective twilight of methodical scepticism and doubt.

That word 'assent' had become particularly important for him, when he was on a holiday in Switzerland in August 1866. He had been working on certitude alone beforehand, and suddenly he knew he was preoccupied with the wrong issue. The mind's act of assent, of saying 'yes' to what one has come to realise is true, was the most important thing – it was 'the clue, the "Open Sesame", of the whole subject'.[1] This when he was at Glion, above Lake Geneva. When he came home, and over the years following, he was therefore able to make good progress, whenever he got the time. Gradually, the book began to take shape. He was rewriting it over and over, towards its conclusion spending weeks at a time on it out at Rednal, until finally in March 1870 it appeared as *An Essay in Aid of a Grammar of Assent*. Despite appearing like a large treatise, and relatively dry in style and content, as its title suggested, the book sold out on the first day of issue, no doubt because of the high regard in which its author was held, so that two further editions had to be printed that year.

The *Grammar of Assent* is in part an exposition of how ordinary people can arrive at certainty about things that are true, even if they may be hard put to demonstrate the validity of their reasoning. The ways in which we reason about things, and try to evaluate and verify, are teased out in the book – and shown to be authentic and real, very personal, and far removed from the dry deductions of logical thought. We are in fact given a capacity for good judgment, which Newman calls the 'illative sense', whereby we can distinguish between what is true and what is not, and arrive at sound and reasonable conclusions. The human mind, through the often virtually unconscious sifting of manifold data, and through the accumulation of probabilities, eventually reaches beyond the level of inference and evaluation, to form a judgment about what really is so, and thereby to assent to what it has come to know to be true.

Everyday life, for Newman, shows the truth of how our minds work, and how we arrive at conclusions, and act on them. By contrast, much in modern philosophy, and in general contemporary thinking, ended up denying how people really think and reason out things. Especially, the English philosophical tradition tended towards rigid patterns of deduction and logical syllogisms, divorced from the actual experience of reasoning, and how people assent to what is true and real. Drained of 'that depth and breadth of associations which constitute their poetry, their rhetoric, and their historical life', words and ideas were separated by logicians from their vibrant human context, becoming just ghosts of themselves, and were starved into dry definitions, far removed from the real 'universal living scene of things'.[2]

The book is an appeal for realism in thought, and an impassioned defence of the human mind and its search for truth. In the midst of the contemporary critical approaches to all received ideas and beliefs,

Newman lays down a challenge to scepticism and its corrosive consequences, arguing on behalf of the human quest for intelligibility and certainty, and basing what he says on the presuppositions of our actual day-to-day reasoning and judgment. On this foundation, he can then go on to justify the reasonableness of religious belief and faith. If philosophical thought only tends towards scepticism in knowing, then of course a rational basis for faith is meaningless, and the modern world's tendency to consider faith as mere credulity or even superstition is justified, leaving one with nothing more than a leap in faith, a leap simply in to the dark. But Newman had spent a lifetime searching for the truth, and he had seen in the long Catholic tradition a great concern for what is objectively true, issuing in a realist philosophy of human knowing, and which exalted the intelligent nature of the life of faith. That faith, existing in learned individuals, and equally in the Birmingham factory girls, was supremely reasonable, even if yet a gift and dependent on the grace and blessing of God.

It is no surprise, then, to find a treatment of conscience at the heart of what Newman has to say. In the young factory workers, or in the educated university people, there is the very same innermost reality of conscience, drawing towards truth, towards what is right, and instilling a sense of guilt when giving way to what is wrong or untruthful. As the deepest place of any person's emotional and intelligent being, Newman believes conscience is also the place of the prompting of God. We are, as he says, 'accustomed to speak of conscience as a voice ... or the echo of a voice, imperative and constraining, like no other dictate in the whole of our experience'.[3] And he elaborates:

> If, as is the case, we feel responsibility, are ashamed, are frightened, at transgressing the voice of conscience, this implies that there is One to whom we are responsible, before whom we are ashamed, whose claims upon us we fear. If, on doing wrong, we feel the same tearful, broken-hearted sorrow which overwhelms us on hurting a mother; if, on doing right, we enjoy the same sunny serenity of mind, the same soothing, satisfactory delight which

follows on our receiving praise from a father, we certainly have within us the image of some person, to whom our love and veneration look, in whose smile we find our happiness, for whom we yearn, towards whom we direct our pleadings, in whose anger we are troubled and waste away. These feelings in us are such as require for their exciting cause an intelligent being …[4]

We are – to put it briefly and directly – before God always, in our innermost self, in our conscience. For Newman, that was the most self-evident and objective truth, to which he had assented since those far off young days of 1816. Conscience is the ground for our existence as human beings, and it is also within us the intimation of the living God.

From all of this, from conscience and the mind's assent to truth, Newman can develop in the *Grammar* an outline of the authentic religious sense in humanity, which he terms Natural religion. Further, he treats of the objective fact of Revelation, shown in scripture, and 'claiming to be received intelligently, by all whom it addresses, as one doctrine, discipline, and devotion directly given from above'.[5] Founded on the Gospel portrayal of Christ and his teaching, Christianity is 'the completion and supplement of Natural Religion, and of previous revelations', as St Paul proclaimed in Athens.[6] This revelation and its Catholic historical realisation 'is a living truth which never can grow old'.[7] It is a teaching and a living religion of universal significance for the world, eliciting the best of our understanding, and of which we can be absolutely sure. Such is Newman's view. He saw that as we can be certain of and assent to many things in everyday life, so we can arrive at this great Catholic certainty about the ultimate truth and meaning of life, handed on through the generations and enduring until the world's end.

The response to the book was naturally varied, with praise coming from a range of people, including the historian James Anthony Froude, and the Anglican theologian James Mozley. Newman was especially pleased to find William George Ward welcoming its approach in the *Dublin Review*, and saying that it was consistent with the views of the best Catholic schoolmen in the past and in more recent times. It was a pleasure for both of them to agree for once on a substantive issue. On the other hand, the Jesuit Thomas Harper, taking a dry, logical and scholastic approach, wrote a series of critical articles on it in *The Month*, to the discomfiture of Henry Coleridge, which led to Newman assuring him, '… if I am to be fried, kinder hands than yours and Father Harper's could not have been selected'.[8] And to Mary Holmes, who of course praised it, he wrote that the last one hundred pages were written 'especially for such ladies as are bullied by infidels and do not know how to answer them – a misfortune which I fear is not rare in this day. I wanted to show that, keeping to broad facts of history, which everyone knows and no one can doubt, there is evidence and reason enough for an honest inquirer to believe in revelation'.[9]

But even while he had been completing the *Grammar*, Newman had been distracted by the larger unfolding Catholic drama – as the Vatican Council was already in session, having opened on 8 December 1869. Further efforts had been made to get him to attend, Bishop Brown of Newport asking him to be his advisor, and later Bishop Dupanloup of Orleans wanting him as his personal theologian. Although honoured by these requests, he felt his place was at home. Still, he was dismayed the concerted efforts of the Ultramontane party to push through the definition of Papal infallibility, led in the Council itself by the powerful and persuasive personality of Manning, and backed up by *The Tablet* under Vaughan, the influential *Univers* of Louis Veuillot in France, and the *Civiltà Cattolica* of the Roman Jesuits, all of whom would brook no opposition to their opinions. So many good Catholics Newman was dealing with, including through correspondence, were upset and confused by the reports of imminent increased Papal authority, and by the bullying Ultramontane accusations thrown at them of disloyalty for not following the extreme authoritarian line.

On 28 January he wrote to Ullathorne in Rome what he remarked later was one of the most passionate and confidential letters he had ever written. Rome 'ought to be a name to lighten the heart at all times,' he said, and yet was now infusing into people 'little else than fear and dismay'. While he like others 'at least practically, not to say doctrinally, hold the Holy Father to be infallible, suddenly there is thunder in the clear sky', with people told to prepare themselves for a great trial, with 'a great difficulty' to be created by the proposed definition. 'What have we done to be treated as the Faithful never were before? ... Why should an aggressive insolent faction be allowed to make the hearts of the just to mourn, whom the Lord hath not made sorrowful?' He remarked that 'some of the truest minds are driven one way and another', and at times are 'angry with the Holy See for listening to the flattery of a clique of Jesuits, Redemptorists and converts'. But he concluded by saying: 'If it is God's will that the Pope's Infallibility should be defined, then it is His Blessed Will to throw back "the times and the moments" of that triumph He has destined for His Kingdom; and I shall feel I have but to bow my head to His Adorable Inscrutable Providence.'[10]

Ullathorne allowed the letter out of his hands for a few hours, and it was copied. In March it appeared in the *Standard* newspaper, and naturally caused a furore, with Ullathorne deeply embarrassed, although Newman in the end glad it had come out. 'Don't mind for me,' he wrote off to Ullathorne, 'I have had too many knocks to care for this.' He continued to think that the definition would be needless, along with a minority group of bishops at the Council, including his friend David Moriarty of Kerry and especially Dupanloup of Orleans. Eventually in July it was defined, and when Newman saw its moderate terms – including the statement that the Pope possessed that infallibility which the Church itself possessed, and which was much less than the Ultramontanes had hoped for – he was pleased. He wondered then about its validity, and believed its guarantee needed the acceptance of the faithful: '... if the definition is eventually received by the whole body of the faithful ... then too it will claim our assent by the force of the great dictum, "Securus judicat orbis terrarum."'[11] Over the time ahead, inevitably, he was in much correspondence with people over the definition, trying to reassure them, and believing that in time what was now unbalanced would be put to right: 'Let us be patient, let us have faith, and a new Pope, and a re-assembled Council may trim the boat.'[12]

Just after the definition the Franco-Prussian War broke out, and the French troops in Rome protecting the Papal States withdrawn.

After a token resistance by the last Papal army, Rome was taken over by the Piedmontese army of King Victor Emmanuel, to complete the unification of Italy, and end the temporal power of the Papacy which had existed since the early middle ages. From now on, the Pope made himself the 'prisoner of the Vatican', with Pius IX paradoxically enjoying unprecedented personal popularity, due in part to his own approachability and winning personality, as well as to the aura around him of a living martyr. The Council itself had adjourned as hostilities began, and was never recalled. As for acceptance of Papal infallibility, soon enough it became clear that all the bishops around the world, including the dissenting ones who had absented themselves from the actual vote on the definition, were submitting to it. As a result, Newman himself was satisfied.

The main casualties were in Germany, where alienated academics went into schism as 'Old Catholics', while separately the ageing Dr Döllinger was excommunicated by the Archbishop of Munich for failing to accept the Council and the definition of Infallibility. In England Lord Acton (he had been created a baron in 1869), who was Döllinger's disciple, managed to avoid excommunication, and remained in the Church. Newman felt Döllinger was treated cruelly, although he had considered for some time that the German's historical approach showed a failure of imagination, being too rigid and anti-Papal, leaving him little room to accept the hierarchical Church's actual mode of operation. And he himself, of course, was once again under a cloud, as a result of the publication of his letter to Ullathorne.

It was to be a while before Newman could speak out publicly. In 1874 William Gladstone's first great Liberal government fell, whose policies had been directed towards 'justice for Ireland'. It had been weakened the year before when his University Bill for Ireland was rejected by the Irish Catholic bishops, their opposition in turn influencing Catholic members of Parliament. In an article, Gladstone blamed the Vatican Council's definition for his defeat, asserting that Catholics could now no longer be loyal citizens. He followed up by publishing in early November a pamphlet, *The Vatican Decrees in their bearing on Civil Allegiance*, of which 150,000 copies were sold by the end of the year. Many people urged Newman to reply to him, including Bishop Brown, Dr Russell of Maynooth, and William Monsell – who had been in Gladstone's administration and was now Lord Emly.

Eventually, from a strong sense of duty Newman realised he must do so – in order once again, as in his earlier reply to Pusey, to dissociate the Church from the extreme views being put forward by Manning and Ward, and which Gladstone had taken as representative of the Catholic position. After some false starts, Newman got down to the most intense writing he had managed since the *Apologia*, working continuously for a month, before finishing his 150-page 'pamphlet' before Christmas, and publishing it on 14 January 1875. Entitled *A Letter to the Duke of Norfolk*, it was addressed to the young Duke who had been a pupil in the Oratory School, and, as a notable Catholic citizen, was an obvious target of Gladstone's criticism.

In his treatment, Newman reminded Gladstone – a good historian, but who was now claiming that Catholics were repudiating ancient history – that Christian history itself, in many notable instances, showed the limits of obedience to the state. This followed from the Church's reliance on its definite message, from the world's own maker. Obedience to the state could not be, and never was, an absolute. And even where obedience to the Church was concerned, Newman brought in the role of conscience, which is 'the voice of God in the nature and heart of man, as distinct from the voice of Revelation'.[13] He rejected the current ideas of conscience as being just a human phenomenon, allowing one the right to do or believe as one pleased. He believed that the Church's authority, and the Pope's authority, rested on God's revelation, which supplemented the natural light of conscience, strengthening it and championing the moral law itself. There could be extreme cases where conscience saw some current order or legislation by the Pope as wrong, and so a person could not obey. But ultimately conscience and the Church's true teaching were in accord, in complementary ways being the voice of God for us.

While he himself accepted the Church's doctrine of infallibility, he wished to set out the historical understanding of it in a moderate and comprehensible way. This he hoped would encourage the many good people who had been unsettled by what appeared to be the novelty of the doctrine as now being promulgated. He did not hesitate to speak out about 'the violence and cruelty' of various publications, which had by their rash language employed themselves 'in unsettling the weak in faith, throwing back inquirers, and shocking the Protestant mind'. Also, 'a feeling was too prevalent in many places that no one could be true to God and His Church, who had any pity on troubled souls, or any scruple of "scandalising those little ones" who believed in Christ, and of "despising and destroying him for whom He died."'[14] In this way, he could not avoid displaying how strongly he felt about the extreme Ultramontanes, and the damage he believed they were inflicting on the Church, and which had led to Gladstone's misunderstanding and the severity of his attack.

As to the Council's decree itself, he said that the revealed message had been entrusted to the Church, and 'so far as the message entrusted to it is concerned, the Church is infallible; for what is meant by infallibility in teaching but that the teacher in his teaching is secured from error?'[15] And, whereas the Catholic faithful ought to have a generous loyalty towards the Church's teaching authority, such a tone of mind in them ought 'to be met and handled with a wise and gentle *minimism*'[16] on the part of that authority.

Much to Newman's surprise, the *Letter to the Duke of Norfolk* was an immediate success, recalling that of the *Apologia* over ten years earlier. It did a great deal to change the public attitude, leading to a greater understanding of the Catholic Church's exercise of its teaching role. Many relieved Catholics wrote to express their gratitude, Emily Bowles speaking for others when she said of a burden lifted, of being regarded as abject subjects or slaves under arbitrary authority. Among the appreciative bishops was Paul Cullen in Dublin, now a cardinal, who gave the *Letter* favourable mention in a pastoral, for which Newman wrote to thank him. And Gladstone was magnanimous in his own response, praising Newman's integrity and 'kindliness of tone', and also, as an admirer of Newman's role in the Oxford Movement, paying tribute to his great importance for the religious history of England.

As for Rome, it seems to have been in two minds, with Cardinal Franchi at Propaganda (who had succeeded to Barnabò) writing to Manning to say that part of Newman's exposition could 'do great harm to the minds of the faithful'. Manning however, aware of the wide acclaim it received, in reply said he was against any '*public*' censure, and added with studied reserve, 'The heart of the revered Fr Newman is as right and as Catholic as it is possible to be'. At least Monsignor Talbot was not around now to add fuel to the smouldering combustible material. Although out of his depth, he had loved to be at the centre of things – but now he was away from Rome, after a breakdown in 1868, and requiring institutional care for the rest of his life at an asylum in Passy, Paris.

Certain points in the *Letter* did continue to rankle in Propaganda, including a sentence of Newman's, that 'the Rock of St Peter on its summit enjoys a pure and serene atmosphere, but there is a great deal of Roman malaria at the foot of it'. The mention of *malaria* was said to be 'troppo irreverente' towards the Roman Curia. Ullathorne in turn was asked to take it on himself to point out the censurable propositions to Newman. But remembering the 'blande suaviterque' secret instruction debacle, he refused this time to do so, passing the responsibility back to Propaganda, which in the event decided to go no further. This year, on the eve of Easter, Manning was made a cardinal. Although he remained suspicious of Newman's loyalty, he continued to leave him alone, allowing him freedom to work within his own sphere.

Life continued on in Birmingham. Now into his seventies, which he had not expected to see, Newman found himself outliving more of his closest friends. Serjeant Bellasis, a friend from Oxford days, and to whom the *Apologia* was dedicated, died in early 1873. Two of his sons would join the Birmingham community. Also that year Henry Wilberforce and James Hope-Scott died, and Newman went to their funerals, both occurring during May. At the end of Henry Wilberforce's Requiem Mass, he was asked to say some words, which he did, holding back his tears. Less than a week later he was the preacher himself at Hope-Scott's Requiem in the Jesuit Church at Farm Street in London. Published in a later edition of *Sermons*

Preached on Various Occasions, as 'In the World, but not of the World', one part of the sermon was devoted to what he called Hope-Scott's 'real inner secret self':

> I cannot do justice by my words to the impression which in this respect he made on me. He had a tender conscience, but I mean something more than that – I mean the emotion of a heart always alive and awake at the thought of God. When a religious question came up suddenly in conversation, he had no longer the manner and the voice of a man of the world. There was a simplicity, earnestness, gravity in his look and in his words, which one could not forget. It seemed to me to speak of a loving desire to please God, a single-minded preference for His service over every service of man, a resolve to approach Him by the way which He had appointed. It was no taking for granted that to follow one's own best opinion was all one with obeying His will; no easy persuasion that a vague, obscure sincerity in our conclusions about Him and our worship of Him was all that was required of us, whether those conclusions belonged to this school of doctrine or that. That is, he had deep within him that gift of which St Paul and St John speak of, when they enlarge upon the characteristics of faith. It was the gift of faith, of a living, loving faith, such as 'overcomes the world' by seeking 'a better country, that is, a heavenly'. This it was that kept him so 'unspotted from the world' in the midst of worldly engagements and pursuits.[17]

Often in London at other times too, he sometimes stayed with Richard Church, after he became Dean of St Paul's in 1871. Richard's children, Helen, Mary and Edith, had been close to him growing up, and had brought him into the world of Lewis Carroll's *Alice's Adventures in Wonderland* and 'The Hunting of the Snark'. He also stayed with Lord John Duke Coleridge, brother of Henry, another Anglican friend of these years. Coleridge's wife, Jane Fortescue Seymour, made by far the best portrait of him in 1873, when he was seventy-three, showing him in a characteristic way leaning his head on his hand, and bringing out his character and captivating presence.

The greatest loss of all came in the wake of the *Letter to the Duke of Norfolk*'s success. Ambrose St John, who had been prone to chronic asthmatic attacks, and seriously overworked for long years, had at Newman's request just translated from the German a balanced book on Papal infallibility by Bishop Fessler, who had been Secretary-General at the Vatican Council. It was all too much, and, just after attending the opening of the Passionist Church of St Mary's in nearby Harborne, his health gave way completely and he died in the night of 24 May 1875, while only in his sixtieth year. Ambrose had been with him since Littlemore, and shared the time in Rome, and had been an unwavering support over all the years since. In a letter to Mary Holmes he summed up what he said in many others: 'This is the greatest affliction I have had in my life, and so sudden. Pray for him and for me.'

After his sermons from the Oxford period were reissued by Copeland, Newman went on publishing again the rest of his Anglican works, and in a uniform edition. In the first of two volumes which he entitled the *Via Media*, he republished his 1837 *Prophetical Office of the Church*, and introduced it with a new and theologically rich preface on the nature of the Church. It was a case of answering his old Anglican self, and correcting former imbalances, such as stressing in isolation the prophetical nature of Christianity, without paying due attention to other necessary aspects. He set out therefore what he saw as the threefold office of Christ shown in scripture, as Prophet, Priest and King. Christ's offices, he asserted, are discharged on earth by the representative he left behind:

> This was Holy church, His mystical Body and Bride, a Divine Institution, and the shrine and organ of the Paraclete, who speaks through her till the end comes. She, to use an Anglican poet's words, is 'His very self below', as far as men on earth are equal to the discharge and fulfilment of high offices, which primarily and supremely are His.[18]

'Christianity, then,' he continued, 'is at once a philosophy, a political power, and a religious rite: as a religion, it is Holy; as a philosophy, it is Apostolic; as a political power, it is imperial, that is, One and Catholic. As a religion, its special centre of action is pastor and flock; as a philosophy, the Schools; as a rule, the Papacy and its Curia.'[19] Each of these offices, he also added, can be inclined to exaggeration, and needs the ministry of the other two for correction and to achieve balance. Thus devotion by itself can tend to superstition, theology to rationalism, and Church power can tend towards ambition and tyranny.

Among the three, theology was singled out for special mention. Newman saw it as 'the fundamental and regulating principle of the whole Church system. It is commensurate with Revelation, and Revelation is the initial and essential idea of Christianity. It is the subject-matter, the formal cause, the expression, of the Prophetical Office, and as being such, has created both the Regal Office and the Sacerdotal'. In a sense, theology even has a power of jurisdiction over the others. Yet here Newman issued a caveat, saying that theology cannot completely have its own way, but 'has to consent to a truce or a compromise, in consequence of the rival force of religious sentiment and ecclesiastical interests'.[20] The three offices or dimensions therefore, in his view, formed a comprehensive wholeness – 'Apostolicity of doctrine and Sanctity of Worship' alongside 'the Regal office'. And they are to be found in the Catholic Church, as nowhere else, in a living interaction within it, despite all its shortcomings.

None of these dimensions, it need hardly be said, were mere ideas for Newman, or for his small group of companions. The daily realities of life in Birmingham had gone on incessantly all these years. For Newman, there were the many visitors, and the enormous correspondence, often occupying him well into the night. In the Oratory he had charge of the library, the accounts and the sacristy. Many hidden things were done for people around, such as providing coal, looking after medical bills, or making sure debts could be cleared in shops. But the more outward works of the large parish area, including the schools and orphanage, the prison and workhouse, had become largely the responsibility of the others. He himself was not unaware of many of the wider social evils of the day and, while ambivalent about some of the movements for social reform, which in his view led to secularism and unbelief, he believed that individuals should be willing to take a stand on social matters. Personally, he was affected by the heartlessness to be found in the prison, and was so committed to the care of the workhouse that he was prepared to limit the work of the parish rather than give it up.

But that realm of worship, consisting of pastor and people, and the manifold care of the flock, was at the heart of things. In the church, there had been further improvements, and its devotional atmosphere was much appreciated. Newman was particularly interested in the music, helping where required, and often as main celebrant continuing to sing the High Mass on the principal feasts. He continued with his hours in the confessional. And when the Blessed Sacrament was exposed, to which his own devotion remained very strong, he liked the flowers surrounding it to be of all kinds and colours, just as he had loved the church at Littlemore to be adorned.

As always, he took his turns in the pulpit to preach. It was remembered long afterwards how he brought out the meaning of scripture for his hearers, speaking in his quiet and expressive way, and more in the manner of conversation than preaching. He spoke *ex tempore*, as was the Catholic custom, the thoughts forming in his mind as he spoke. He had a small Bible in his hands, from which he often quoted, turning over the pages as he spoke on, in order to find the next passage to be mentioned. This was because he had grown up with the Authorised Version, and wished to quote correctly from the Catholic Rheims-Douay Bible. Very occasionally, he made some notes beforehand. But his usual custom was afterwards to write down for himself notes on what he had said. These were eventually collected and published posthumously, in 1913, as the *Sermon Notes of John Henry Cardinal Newman, 1849–1878*.

Quietly, too, his own devotion to the Oratory remained as steadfast as ever. His larger hopes for its expansion had not materialised. While the very separate London group had gone on successfully, all the signs were that his own diminished Birmingham Oratory might not survive after him. Yet he worked on, as Superior having the ultimate responsibility for everything in it, and with steadfast faith that God would provide. After the *Apologia,* two novices came, John Norris in 1865, and the fifty-year-old Thomas Pope in 1867, after the deaths of his wife and children. Then there were no more for a time. Only after the death of Ambrose St John did the real change come, and the future begin to look bright. In March 1877 Newman wrote to Maria Giberne (who years back had joined the Visitation sisters at Autun in France): 'I think Ambrose is helping us, who was so anxious that we had no novices. Now we have four, and the prospect of three more.' Among them were the two sons of Serjeant Bellasis, Richard and Henry, as well as the Oxford scholar Thomas Eaglesim. Another was Francis Morgan, who is perhaps best known as the later Oratorian guardian of J.R.R. Tolkien.

NOTES

1. *LD*, XXV, p. 199.
2. *GA*, pp. 267–8.
3. Ibid., p. 107.
4. Ibid., pp. 109–10.
5. Ibid., p. 387.
6. Ibid., p. 388.
7. Ibid., p. 487.
8. *LD*, XXV, p. 98.
9. Ibid., p. 68.
10. Ibid., pp. 18–19.
11. Ibid., pp. 164–5; and *Diff,* p. 303.
12. *LD*, XXV, p. 310.
13. *Diff,* p. 247.
14. Ibid., p. 300.
15. Ibid., p. 323.
16. Ibid., p. 339.
17. *SVO*, pp. 275–6.
18. *VM*, I, p. xxxix.
19. Ibid., p. xl.
20. Ibid., pp. xlvii–xlix.

— CHAPTER II —

And a Cardinal

IN DECEMBER 1877 Oxford surprisingly entered into his life again, when Newman received an invitation from the President of his original college, Trinity, to become its first Honorary Fellow. He replied at once: 'No compliment could I feel more intimately, or desire more eagerly at once to seize and appropriate than that which is the subject of your letter just received. Trinity College is now, and ever has been, in my habitual thoughts.' He asked for time, however, to consult on whether he could accept the honour, and then wrote to Ullathorne for his advice, in view of the hierarchy's continuing opposition to mixed education in places like Oxford. Finding Ullathorne in favour, he wrote to accept the invitation. He was delighted to be returning to Trinity, and had never wavered in his affection for the place, where in company with John Bowden he had started out on his long career. It was as if he was now to end his life as he had begun, as a member of Trinity.

Meanwhile in early January Edward Caswall died, having struggled on with a bad heart for some time. He was buried at Rednal alongside Ambrose St John and Joseph Gordon, all three having been, for Newman, 'the life and centre of the Oratory'. Across from them was the grave of Frances Wootten, who had died in January 1876, and whose place in the school had been taken by Emily Bowles.

Newman's visit to Oxford took place in February, his first since spending that last night in the house of Manuel Johnson, in the same month of February, thirty-two years before. In the company of William Neville, also a Trinity man, he stayed a few days. As well as dining with the fellows and having lunch with the President, he visited Oriel, and met with Pusey, and went to see the new college named after Keble. He did not get out to Littlemore. But later in the year, during September, he repaired the omission, when he went down to Oxford again by himself. He travelled out to visit the house of his mother and sisters at Iffley, where he met its current occupants – and then, as he told Jemima's sister-in-law Anne Mozley, 'I went boldly into my Mother's garden and was amazed how beautiful forty years had made it'. Afterwards he walked on to Littlemore, before returning to Birmingham in the evening.

At the beginning of 1878, too, the longest Pontificate in history was drawing to a close. Cardinal Manning had gone to Rome, and for five weeks was by the side of Pius IX during his final illness, until he died on 7 February. Pope Leo XIII succeeded him, who was quite a different figure, and intellectually brilliant, although already nearly sixty-eight years of age. Signalling that his policy towards the modern world would be more positive, it seems that early on he wished to make Newman his first cardinal. In England, the matter was taken up separately by some among the Catholic community, and especially by the Duke of Norfolk, who believed that Rome should honour Newman in this way. Approached by Norfolk, along with Lord Petre and the Marquis of Ripon, Manning then agreed to petition the new Holy Father to this effect, and wrote a generous recommendation. But it was the Duke of Norfolk himself, who in December first made Leo XIII personally aware of the wishes of eminent lay Catholics. Newman himself had only heard rumours about the matter in the summer, and dismissed them as highly unlikely.

It was towards the end of January 1879 that word came from Rome, enquiring whether Newman would be prepared to become a cardinal. Ullathorne, as his Bishop, strongly urged him to accept. Overwhelmed, frail in health, Newman was in a dilemma about what to do, as cardinals were required to live in Rome if they were not diocesan bishops. So in consultation with Ullathorne he wrote in reply, expressing his great appreciation of the offer being made, but asking that he might be allowed to end his days in his 'much loved Oratory'. He did not want to be seen as making a condition, and trying to bargain with the Pope. His letter was addressed to Ullathorne, and was to be sent on to Rome by Cardinal Manning, with a covering letter from Ullathorne himself making it clear that Newman wanted to accept the honour. All at once Ullathorne became suspicious about what Manning might do, and immediately sent him a second letter of explanation, reinforcing the point of Newman's acceptance. Manning however ignored what Ullathorne said in his two letters, and took it upon himself to decide that Newman had refused. He was going to Rome himself at that time, and sent ahead Newman's letter by itself, without Ullathorne's covering explanation as requested.

Soon the story was put out, including in the *Times*, that Newman had refused the Red Hat. It took strong letters from both the Duke of Norfolk and Newman himself to Manning, who had reached Rome, before Manning altered his approach. To his credit, he then immediately informed Leo XIII that Newman wished to accept the cardinalate, who was delighted, and exempted him from the requirement of living in Rome. The official letter appointing him reached Newman on 18 March, who told his community, 'The cloud has lifted from me for ever'. 'It puts an end to all those reports,' he also wrote, 'that my teaching is not Catholic or my books trustworthy, which has been so great a trial to me for so long.' He knew that a refusal on his part, which some had wanted including Anglican friends, would have been ungracious to the Pope, reinforcing the view that he was only a half-Catholic, and would have upset those who wanted his name vindicated.

Letters of congratulation poured in, and all his energies were used in replying to them. On 4 April he was in London to receive an address from the Irish Catholic MPs, the first of many he was to receive in the months ahead. Soon afterwards he was off to Rome, accompanied by William Neville, arriving there after a week of travel on 24 April. Just as he was about to go down with a severe cold he met the Pope, who received him 'most affectionately', and enquired especially about his community. Afterwards he was laid up, and had to turn down invitations, and abandon plans to have a number of conversations with some cardinals and with the Holy Father.

Yet someone far away was very much on his mind. William Froude had lost his wife Catherine, herself always close and loving towards Newman, on 24 July the year before, while they were out in India. Grief-stricken by her death, Froude travelled to South Africa, and had written from there to Newman about his own still unresolved issues around religious certainty. Newman now in Rome, confined to his room, began drafting a very long letter in reply, appealing even to his engineer's mind, while also hoping that the prayers of his beloved departed wife might finally aid her husband's journey into Catholic faith. Sadly, it was never sent, as word arrived that William had unexpectedly died from dysentery.

On 14 May Newman had recovered enough to go out and receive from the Secretary of State the *biglietto*, informing him that he had been elevated to the College of Cardinals. The speech he gave in reply was a great reiteration of all he had fought for over his life, about seeking the truth in religious matters, and opposing the old foe of religious liberalism, as 'the doctrine that there is no positive truth in religion'. He spoke of the rise of infidelity, the 'great *apostasia*' in society, the contemporary 'throwing off' of Christianity, especially in his own country of England, and which was giving rise to immense challenges for the future. Yet he also reminded his hearers of the continuing work of Providence in the midst of all things. As for the Church, commonly she 'has nothing more to do than go on in her own proper duties, in confidence and peace; to stand still and see the salvation of God'.[1]

For his motto he took the phrase '*Cor ad cor loquitur*', 'Heart speaks to heart', and which was from St Francis de Sales, whose humanism and gentle spirit he greatly admired. A few days after his *biglietto* speech, he received the cardinal's hat at a public consistory. As he related himself, the 'wonderful attention' he received from Leo XIII 'astonished all there'. Then his cold developed into pneumonia, and he was laid up once again. When he recovered, and set out for home, he had to forgo a cherished wish to visit the excommunicated Dr Döllinger in Munich. He was sick again at Leghorn, and was laid up for a week. Afterwards once again he had to change his plans, being ordered to abandon a detour to see Maria Giberne at her convent in Autun. He arrived back at Folkestone on 27 June, and was able to make several calls at Brighton, including to Mary Wilberforce, whose husband William died while he was away. Diverting from there, he went to visit a delighted Bloxam, who was Rector of Upper Beeding Anglican Church, in Sussex. And on 1 July he arrived back at Birmingham's New Street Station, to be met by a large crowd. Not to disappoint his parishioners, he changed into the cardinal's vestments presented to him by the lay Catholic Union, before arriving at the Oratory church by cab, for an improvised ceremony, and simply telling everyone, in a little speech as he sat leaning his head on his hand, 'It is such happiness to come *home*'.

Much of his energies were then taken up responding to addresses and congratulations, including many from Ireland. He paid another visit to Oxford, mainly to present his collection of Keble's letters to Keble College. Four of his Anglican friends, Rogers (now Lord Blachford), Copeland, Church and Lord Coleridge, combined to get him a small carriage, discreetly emblazoned with his cardinal's coat of arms. In May of 1880 he travelled to a major reception at Norfolk House in London, where among others he met Matthew Arnold, the brother of Tom, and the illustrious author of *Culture and Anarchy* and *The Scholar Gypsy*. Staying at Norfolk House, he also found it possible to visit the Brompton Oratory, despite the estrangement, because of his new status. On a second visit there from Norfolk House, he received two hundred of the clergy. Later that month he had more 'triumphant processions' (as Frederic Rogers called them), when he spent some days back at Oxford again, and preached twice on Trinity Sunday in the new Jesuit Church of St Aloysius, with Henry Coleridge presiding. It was all such a change for him, and due to the new atmosphere brought into the Church by Leo XIII. Years later the Pope told an English visitor: 'My Cardinal! It was not easy, it was not easy. They said he was too liberal, but I had determined to honour the Church in honouring Newman. I always had a cult for him. I am proud that I was able to honour such a man.'

When matters quietened down he managed to resume life in the Oratory, much as before. He was not allowed to continue in the confessional, but he still took his turns at preaching, until eventually his voice became too weak to be heard. Along with his correspondence, he also worked to complete the republication of his Anglican works. He had been making an extensive revision of his two volumes on his patristic hero St Athanasius, until interrupted by the Cardinalate. Now he was able to take up the task again, and kept at them on and off until they were ready to go to press.

On Christmas Day 1879, he had received a telegram with the news that Jemima had died. Her husband John had predeceased her some years earlier, and Newman had been anxious to help her afterwards, offering advice on business and financial matters to her and her daughter Janie. He sorely missed Jemima now, but kept up a good correspondence with Anne Mozley. His brother Frank called from time to time, but they had little in common, except perhaps earlier when helping their impecunious brother Charles. Remaining always an atheistic socialist, and never managing to hold down a job for long, Charles had been living a reclusive existence for some twenty-five years at Tenby, on the southern Pembrokeshire coast of Wales, mainly supported by Frank. Hearing he was ill, his eldest brother tried to call on him in September 1882. He stayed overnight in a hotel, and then made his way out from the town, to the cottages where Charles lived, on the windswept edge of a salt marsh. But he seems to have been turned away. A landlady and her daughter had been looking after Charles, and, after the lady's death, the daughter continued her devotion. When Charles died in 1884, John Henry had his gravestone erected, and with the text: 'Despise not O Lord the work of Thy hands.'

Others had departed at this time. In February 1880 Charles Russell died in Ireland, having been President of Maynooth for long years. Newman, writing to his Jesuit nephew, Fr Matthew Russell, expressed how much he owed to him. Then in the same month when he tried to make contact with Charles, there occurred the death of Edward Bouverie Pusey. There had been immense suffering in Pusey's life, and yet extraordinary achievements, especially in bringing about the Catholic revival in Anglicanism. Despite some contradictory aspects to his character, he was, as Newman always saw, a person of true greatness and undoubted personal holiness. At his funeral, 'Lead Kindly Light' was sung. A short while later, Richard Church spoke of him from Newman's old pulpit of St Mary's in Oxford: 'No man was more variously judged, more sternly condemned, more tenderly loved … First and foremost, he was one who lived his life, as above everything, the Servant of God.'

Once again, despite these further losses, life moved on. Early on as a cardinal, Newman hoped to make a return visit to Rome, to use his new influence there in urging free discussion on important theological subjects, and to advocate a more enlightened policy on Catholic education. Such approaches on the part of the Church would inspire confidence in thoughtful people, and strengthen them in withstanding 'the intellectual flood that is setting in against Christianity'. But his health remained too fragile for him to go. All he could do eventually was send a letter with a delegation going to Rome, headed by the young convert Lord Braye, to discuss educational matters. In the letter, which was passed to the Pope, he pleaded for a change of policy towards Oxford. With Pusey gone now, there was little influence left in Oxford, of a properly religious and Catholic nature, to stem the tide of Liberal thought. It would be only after Newman's own death when Rome lifted the general ban on Catholics attending the national universities.

A few other intellectual challenges came his way. For long he had been concerned with the historicity of the Bible and its interpretation, and in the light of new scientific discoveries, but had felt unable to publish anything about the matter. So he now wrote an article for *The Nineteenth Century*, on 'Inspiration in its Relation to Revelation', and which appeared in February 1884. It was a modest but pioneering attempt to move away from biblical literalism and allow for the independence of scientific thought. Dr John Healy of Maynooth, writing soon after in the *Irish Ecclesiastical Record*, was fiercely critical of the 'startling character' of the article. This in turn led to a robust reply from Newman, who termed Healy 'a not over-courteous, nor over-exact writer … Had he not been in a hurry to publish, he would have made a better Article. I took above a twelve-month for mine'.[2] Later in the year, when Dr Healy was made

Coadjutor Bishop of Clonfert, Newman sent him a specially bound copy of the Roman Canon, and received in return a grateful and also contrite letter.

A final controversy was with a young Congregationalist theologian, Dr A.M. Fairbairn, on the relationship of faith and reason, with Fairbairn accusing Newman of distrusting the power of reason, and promoting scepticism in his writings. Newman took great pains in replying to what he considered were serious misrepresentations of his position. He admitted that he had sometimes used the word 'reason' in a derogatory sense, as for instance 'Reason in fact and concretely in fallen man', 'Reason in the educated intellect of England, France and Germany', Reason in 'every Government and every civilisation through the world which is under the influence of the European mind', and which needed its 'stiff neck bent'. But in itself, the gift of reasoning, and our desire to understand, and to reach towards the truth, is good. This he had learned from the philosophy of Aristotle, above all, who had taught him to call it 'the *noetic* faculty'. And of course he had tried to outline its use, alongside that of the moral sense, or conscience, especially in the *Grammar of Assent*. Newman's rejoinders were published in an article, 'The Development of Religious Error', in the *Contemporary Review* for October 1885, and in an important postscript, added when he reprinted the article privately the next year.[3]

During 1884 and 1885 Newman followed with anguished interest the war in Egypt and Sudan. He especially felt for General Gordon, and was deeply upset when he was killed two days before a relief expedition arrived in Khartoum. Later, he was amazed to learn that Gordon had with him in Khartoum a copy of the *Dream of Gerontius*, in which he had marked his favourite passages. Gordon had passed it to the *Times* correspondent Frank Power, who sent it to his sister in Ireland, Mrs Mary Murphy, before being killed himself. She then sent it to Birmingham for Newman's inspection. It took his breath away. What struck him most about Gordon's use of the *Dream*, Newman wrote to a friend, was that 'in St Paul's words he "died daily"; he was always on his deathbed, fulfilling the common advice that we should ever pass the day as if it were our last'.

When in London he still stayed with Richard Church, in the deanery of St Paul's Cathedral. And when his fingers failed him on the lovely violin presented years ago by Church and Rogers, he passed it on to Richard's daughter Mary. He helped Church, too, as he was preparing his classic account of the Oxford Movement. Church wrote about seeing in him 'the obstinate preference for reality over show, however tempting – with the wholesome power of being able to think little about oneself'. Again he stayed with Lord and Lady Coleridge (Jane Fortescue). Coleridge wrote in 1882: 'I cannot analyse it or explain it, but to this hour he interests and awes me like no other man I ever saw. He is as simple and humble as a child, and, yet, I am with a being unlike anyone else'. Many others, too, spoke of those extraordinary personal qualities of his, which captivated them, and which seem to have increased as he grew older.

Cardinal Manning however was unable to change his views about Newman. He believed to the end that he was a disloyal Catholic, whose writings contained dangerous heresies. On one occasion he had an animated row with Ullathorne, telling him he was no match for Newman, who 'simply twists you round his little finger'. The Yorkshireman replied by standing up for Newman, and, as he related it, telling Manning pointedly that 'there was no honester man on earth; that his only aim on this earth was to advance the cause of religion; that his deep humility forced him to come to the surface to show his sincerity; that he was an avowed hater of duplicity and intrigue, and much more to the purpose'. Manning would remain at a distance from Newman, in his own wide circle of influence, and with his legitimate claim to fame resting on his work for the children of poor Catholics, and on his influential concern for social justice, carried over from his Anglican days.

In Birmingham, Newman's last years were lived out in the relative seclusion of the Oratory. Birmingham had grown enormously during his time there, gathering all the municipal trappings of a great modern city, until finally granted that official status in 1889. Newman's connections with it at a civic level were minimal. But after he was made a cardinal he was invited to be one of the Vice-Presidents of its famous Triennial Music Festival, a post he held on three occasions, attending rehearsals as well as the actual performances in the Town Hall. While often the more recent composers were represented there, he preferred the ones he had known when young, especially Handel, Mozart and Beethoven. He thought Wagner for instance all 'sound and fury'. But hearing Cherubini's *Mass in C* for the first time in 1879, he was very taken, and had it performed twice later in the Oratory, in 1886. Beethoven remained his greatest love: 'I used to call him the gigantic nightingale. He is like a great bird singing.' He was not to hear Elgar's beautiful rendering of his own *Dream of Gerontius*, which was first performed at the 1900 Music Festival.

Having given up the violin, he was soon to find his writing more and more difficult. 'I write slowly and with pain,' he would say, or 'Excuse my handwriting. I am now scarcely able to form any letters'. Still he went on, but the great correspondence was gradually diminishing. He kept up with everyone he had known, writing shorter and more pithy letters, and still answered enquirers and controversialists, many of them Protestant and Evangelical. To Maria Giberne, as her health was failing, he wrote: 'You are, I know, in our Lord's loving hands. You have given yourself to a life of great penance for His sake, and He will not, does not, forget it'. An interesting letter in March 1887 was to Gerard Manley Hopkins, over in Dublin, teaching Classics in the Jesuit-run University College on St Stephen's Green. Against a background of rural anarchy at the time, and anti-English sentiment, Hopkins had written expressing his dismay. Newman felt for him, but in reply said: 'There is one consideration however which you omit. The Irish Patriots hold that they never have yielded themselves to the sway of England and therefore never have been under her laws, and never have been rebels ... If I were an Irishman, I should be (in heart) a rebel ... My fingers will not let me write more'.[4]

For years he had been sorting his correspondence, and with a view to its eventual use by whoever would care to tell the story of his times. In 1884 he handed over his Anglican material to Anne Mozley, who had produced an edition of the letters of her theologian brother James. She was delighted to get to work, and eventually produced in 1891 the substantial two-volume *Letters and Correspondence of John*

Henry Newman during his Life in the English Church. For himself, the memories he kept were increasing, as names were entered into his little anniversary book, with its cross-stitched cover made long ago by Pusey's wife Maria during her last illness, the first name in it being her baby christened by Newman, and who had died early. Soon his old curate Copeland was dying: 'My very dear Copeland, God be your strength and your life, my very dear friend', Newman wrote to him. And Maria Giberne died far away in her convent at Autun, in December 1885, whose association and friendship went back to the family days in Brighton, and to the time when Mary died. All were remembered, including his former Littlemore parishioners, and prayed for at Mass.

For as long as he could, he kept up his routine at the Oratory, taking part in its day-to-day life, still receiving visitors, and pleased with the new and younger generation in the community, who in turn were devoted to him. Among them now was the young Denis Sheil, nephew of the Irish politician Richard Lalor Sheil, and who would be the Oratorian with the longest memory of Newman, living until 1962. Inevitably, however, those around Newman could see how old age was taking its toll. From 1886 onwards he was obviously weakening. He began losing his sight, so that William Neville, who was constantly by his side, was more and more writing his dictated letters from later 1887 onwards. His last sermon was on New Year's Day, 1888, at the celebration of Leo XIII's Golden Jubilee as a priest. He remarked on how the Pope had been an old and comparatively unknown man when elected: 'There did not seem any likelihood that he would leave his Perugian bishopric, but he was found as others were found, by the special providence and inspiration of God, and we in our ignorance knew nothing about him.'

The last three meetings with Ullathorne were in this period, the final one being at the Dominican convent in Stone, to which Newman travelled in July 1888, on the way to a short holiday touring North Wales. Ullathorne had retired the previous March, and became a titular Archbishop. The community were delighted to see the two together, the weaker Newman leaning on Ullathorne's arm, and Ullathorne pouring out his tea. That October Newman fell, and was knocked unconscious, but against expectations managed to recover. He was too unwell, and still in shock, to receive a visit from Gladstone the next month, but managed a few words to him in his own hand: 'I have known and admired you so long. But I can't write nor talk nor walk and hope you will take my blessing which I give from my heart.'[5]

It was Ullathorne who went first, dying in March 1889, Newman able to be present at his funeral in St Chad's, before the funeral cortege departed for the burial at the convent in Stone, near the grave of Margaret Hallahan. In September, Newman congratulated Manning on settling the dockers' strike in London, and pleasant letters passed between them. Later that month, Frederic Rogers wrote to tell him he was seriously ill himself, and would not recover. 'God bless you, ever and always', were Newman's words to him. In November, he went out in the snow to Bournville, to negotiate with the Quaker George Cadbury and his brother for the separate provision of prayers for the young Catholic women working in their large chocolate manufactuary. On 21 November Rogers died, his widow Lady Blachford writing to Newman that very day. His was a great loss, being the last of the earlier and very close Oxford group of friends. And on Christmas Day that year he said his own last Mass. With sight and strength greatly failed, he was afraid of an accident should he continue. But he learned by heart a Mass of the Blessed Virgin and a Mass for the Dead, reciting one or other of these daily.

In January 1890 he dictated a letter to a Mr George T. Edwards, an Evangelical correspondent, and included his own translation of the prayer 'Soul of Christ':

> My dear Mr Edwards, – Accept my tardy Christmas greetings and good wishes to you for fullness of faith, hope, charity, gladness and peace; for the blessings of Holy Church, and of Gospel gifts, for the Communion of Saints, and the Life Everlasting.
>
> I shall venture to send you what I may call my Creed over-leaf. Yours most truly, J.H.N.

My Creed:
Soul of Christ, be my sanctification;
Body of Christ, be my salvation;
Blood of Christ, fill all my veins;
Water of Christ's side, wash out my stains,
Passion of Christ, my comfort be,
O good Jesus, listen to me
In Thy wounds I fain would hide
Ne'er to be parted from Thy side;
Guard me should the foe assail me;
Call me when my life shall fail me.
Bid me come to Thee above,
With Thy Saints to sing Thy love,
World without end. Amen.[6]

On 21 February he entered into his ninetieth year. When the Oratory school holidays came in July 1890 he was in animated form, talking with everyone, giving out the prizes, and attending the play in the evening. But he could become quite depressed and lonely whenever he felt shut up in his room all day, with nothing to do. Poor anxious Neville sometimes tried too hard to be of help, leading to a gentle rejoinder: 'I am not capable of doing anything more – I am not wanted – now mind what I say, it is not kind to wish to keep me longer from God.' And he was not pleased when the doctors spoke of him living a year or two more, when he knew his time was much nearer.

Over all those months he was still dictating letters to a range of correspondents. His last letter was on 2 August 1890, to his estranged sister Harriet's only child, Grace Langford. Last seen by him when she was aged three, in 1843, she had married and gone to Australia, and now was back on a visit and hoped to meet him. 'My dear Grace,' he said, 'Thank you for your wish to see me. I embrace it readily and I will see you whatever day next week suits you for that purpose. Yours affectionately J.H.N. PS. I am sometimes engaged with the doctor.'[7] So Grace came after all those years, on 9 August, and he held her hand while they talked together.

That evening he caught a chill, and even though he rose the next morning, which was Sunday, he had to go to bed again. He had pneumonia, and seemed to know he was dying. Over thirty years before, when he was at his lowest, feeling put aside – and quite impoverished himself, though he hid the fact – a poor woman had left him a silk scarf with a message of respect. He had kept it carefully. Now he had it brought to him, and put it on, although the doctors could not see the need. He asked Neville to recite the Divine Office with him that day. He was unconscious most of the next day, and received just the anointing of Extreme Unction, but not Holy Communion. He died that evening, at quarter to nine, on Monday, 11 August 1890.

Down in Sussex, on receiving a telegram with the news, Bloxam flew the flag of St George at half-mast over his church, and tolled the bell until the day of the funeral. In the Jesuits, Henry Coleridge, now paralysed, had already heard on the Sunday evening 'that it was feared that the lapse of a few hours would make us orphans of him whom so many of us had been wont to love and revere as the father of our souls'. He burst into tears that Monday night when word came of the end. And William Monsell, his closest Irish friend and supporter, and devoted disciple for more than fifty years, made arrangements like many others to come for the obsequies. In the Oratory church, the body was placed in an open coffin, and great numbers of people from Birmingham and elsewhere filed past. Even as different a character as Lord Rosebery, future Liberal Prime Minister, travelled to view what he believed were a saint's remains, and bent down to kiss the ring on his finger. He related: 'And this was the end of the young Calvinist, the Oxford don, the austere Vicar of St Mary's. It seemed as if a whole cycle of human thought and life were concentrated in that august repose. That was my overwhelming thought. Kindly light had led and guided Newman to this strange, brilliant, incomparable end.'

At his Requiem Mass on Tuesday, 19 August, a huge congregation attending overflowed out along the Hagley Road. Among the mourners were the Mozleys, including Anne, as well as the Duke of Norfolk, Lords Coleridge and Emly (William Monsell), the President of Trinity in Oxford, the Provost of Oriel, the Dean of Durham, and

Tom Arnold. As the cortege afterwards went on its way to Rednal, great numbers lined the route, up to twenty thousand. Out on that eastern-facing side of the Lickey Hills, he was quietly buried in the same grave as his dearest friend, Ambrose St John, and near to the others, Joseph Gordon, Robert Aloysius Boland, Edward Caswall and Frances Wootten. The pall over the coffin was embroidered with his motto, '*Cor ad cor loquitur*', 'Heart speaks to heart'. And in the Oratory, on his memorial tablet were placed his own chosen words, '*Ex umbris et imaginibus in veritatem*' – 'Out of the images and shadows and into the truth'.

NOTES

1. cf. William Neville (ed.), *Addresses to Cardinal Newman with his Replies*, London: Longmans, Green and Co., 1905, pp. 64–9; and text on website: www.newmanreader.org 'Newman Reader – Works of John Henry Newman', *Biglietto Speech* (1879).

2. Texts in J. Derek Holmes and Robert Murray (eds), *On the Inspiration of Scripture*, London: Geoffrey Chapman, 1967; and on website: www.newmanreader.org 'Newman Reader – Works of John Henry Newman'.

3. Texts on website: www.newmanreader.org 'Newman Reader – Works of John Henry Newman'.

4. *LD*, XXXI, p. 195.

5. Ibid., p. 266.

6. Ibid., pp. 281–2.

7. Ibid., p. 299.

— IN RETROSPECT —

THE LEGACY LEFT by Newman is a lasting one. At the time of his death, numerous efforts were made to assess the significance of his life and thought, and from very different points of view. Cardinal Manning, unable to attend the funeral in Birmingham because of frail health, paid a fine public tribute at the Brompton Oratory soon afterwards, despite his own private viewpoint, saying that 'for no one in our memory has such a heartfelt and loving veneration been poured out … Someone has said, whether Rome canonises him or not, he will be canonised in the thoughts of pious people of many creeds in England'. Henry Coleridge, in a particularly profound article entitled 'A Father of Souls' in *The Month*, wrote about the care for truth in the whole course of his life: 'Here was a man who had always told the truth, sought the truth before all things, who had sacrificed everything for the sake of the truth, and who would never deceive any one, or for any consideration whatever swerve an inch from the path of truth.' And he mentioned the respect that had grown for him among so many:

It was not a sentiment or admiration for his many virtues, still less was it the classical beauty or the masculine force of his style, that made Englishmen believe in him and trust him. He had all these and other gifts of the kind, but it was above all because truth was for him the one thing in the world to live for and to die for.[1]

And Richard Church, in the *Guardian's* obituary, wrote from the perspective of Anglicanism:

> Cardinal Newman is dead, and we lose in him not only one of the very greatest masters of English style, not only a man of singular purity and beauty of character, not only an eminent example of personal sanctity, but the founder, we may almost say, of the Church of England as we see it. What the Church of England would have become without the Tractarian Movement, we can faintly guess, and of the Tractarian Movement Newman was the living soul and the inspiring genius. Great as his services have been to the communion in which he died, they are as nothing by the side of those he rendered to the communion in which the most eventful years of his life were spent … He will be mourned by many in the Roman Church, but their sorrow will be less than ours, because they have not the same paramount reason to be grateful to him.[2]

Yet, as the years and decades went by, nothing was more evident than his great influence on the evolving thought and theology of Catholicism itself. As a writer in the *Cork Examiner* stated in 1890: 'A century, at least, must elapse before men shall be in a position to consider with adequate appreciation the nobility, the blessedness of John Henry Newman's character.'[3] It would require the work of many theologians, as the twentieth century unfolded, and then the great debates within and around the Second Vatican Council (1962–65), together with the promulgation of its documents, to bring out the prophetic significance of all he had tried to articulate and stand for during his own lifetime.

Regarding his personal character, a long period would pass before a true picture was presented to a wider public. The extremely damaging portrait of him, concerning his supposed 'supersensitivity', first put out in Catholic London circles in the 1850s and 1860s, has had long-lasting effects. When the otherwise excellent two-volume study by Wilfrid Ward, *The Life of John Henry Cardinal Newman*, came out in 1912, this picture was to some extent presented again. The Birmingham Oratorians were taken aback by what was shown there – for, although Ward (son of his Ultramontane opponent W.G. Ward) displayed the great range of Newman's mind, his portrayal of him as rather sad, at least in later life, was quite a surprise. It was a portrait which did not accord with what his former companions had known, of the down-to-earth, strong and often humorous person they had lived side-by-side with every day. It took the monumental two-volume biography by Meriol Trevor, *Newman: The Pillar of the Cloud*, and *Newman: Light in Winter*, published as late as 1962, to put the record straight and show the wholesomeness and courage of his character. Sometimes the distortion still persists. This is not to deny the occasions when he was afflicted by sadness – above all when he advanced in age, and when so many friends extremely dear to him had departed. And he certainly had a real sensitivity – but it was that of a very intelligent human being, possessed of deep feeling, and with an uncommon care for truth. The whole story of his life shows this.

Some works of Newman were published posthumously. His *Sermon Notes 1849–1878* (1913) has been mentioned already. Others included the beautiful *Meditations and Devotions* (1893), *Autobiographical Writings* (1956), and his Oratorian papers in *Newman the Oratorian*, by Dom Placid Murray of Glenstal Abbey (1969). But over all the years since his death, there were the continuing efforts to gather and collate his letters. It was with the advantage of access to most of these that Meriol Trevor could write her in some ways still unsurpassed account of his life. Eventually, in one of the most extraordinary of publishing enterprises ever attempted, these have seen the light of day, as the *Letters and Diaries of John Henry Newman*, forming thirty-two volumes issued between 1961 and 2008. There especially we meet the living and breathing Newman, in all the range of his personality and interests, in his relationships with so many people, in his concern for them, and his encouragement in matters of faith.

Much could be outlined on his spirituality and prayer, and yet perhaps it is best to have said little. The quotations in the following appendix will show something of that spirit. It may not be far-fetched to say that, in line with a very young and unknown contemporary of his later years, St Thérèse of Lisieux, he believed in the spirituality of the ordinary and hidden things of life. Although of great mind himself, to those who knew him best, like Margaret Hallahan, he was simple and humble, and always conscious of being before God. William Neville, for instance, used Newman's own words to describe him in this latter regard: 'His was a life of prayer. The works and ways of God, the mercies of Christ, the real purpose and uses of this life, the unseen things of the spiritual world, were always uppermost in his mind. His speech and conversation showed it.' Interestingly, these were words spoken back in 1828, when he was young, at the funeral of his own original spiritual mentor, the Evangelical clergyman Walter Mayers.

As for his vision, something of it has been outlined in this account. There are endless books and articles to which one can turn to understand more about his philosophical and theological concerns. Some of the books are mentioned in the bibliography at the end. Of all his works, it could be said that many of his Anglican sermons remain outstanding, among the *Parochial and Plain Sermons* and the *University Sermons*. They are the compositions of a poet, in prose language. Those preached in Dublin can be rated with them. And the *Development of Doctrine*, the *Idea of a University*, the *Apologia pro Vita Sua* and the *Grammar of Assent* rank in their different ways as classics. And yet 'classics' is not quite the word, as with the *Development* and *Idea* and *Grammar* he believed he was simply opening up aspects of the various subjects he treated. Many others have continued since where he left off – although often they have found themselves returning to him once more, to find further inspiration and insight.

He would have rejoiced in the Second Vatican Council, and in effect had hoped for it. His words after the First Vatican Council, 'Let us be patient, let us have faith, and a new pope, and a re-assembled Council may trim the boat', were in their way prophetic. There came eventually John XXIII, elected Pope in 1958, and soon his call to assemble a great Ecumenical Council. And if Newman has often been described as a prophet of Vatican II, it is because he had fought for the same kind of wide and great vision set forth by that Council. He would have admired the courageous theologians whose previous labours led to its major documents, people like Yves Congar and Henri de Lubac, and also outstanding prelates like Cardinal Suenens of Malines-Brussels and Cardinal König of Vienna, alongside many more who were open to the riches of the Christian proclamation, and the never-ending challenge to engage with the modern world's questions and needs.

The world of ecumenical endeavour has moved on considerably since his time. In the Church under Pius IX, and indeed later, the need for interchurch dialogue was hardly recognised. Certain Anglicans wished for it, and some Catholics too, but not the official Catholic Church. It took the efforts of many far-seeing people in the twentieth century, and the vision of Vatican II itself, to change that perspective, although further challenges have been posed in recent years. Perhaps it is not out of place to suggest that Newman's continuously lively mind would have been prepared to see new aspects to how Christians can be drawn together in mind and heart – and beyond what was thought possible in his nineteenth century.

In any case, it is right to say that Newman's name ought always to be linked with John Keble's, and with that of Edward Bouverie Pusey. Further, it is clear that it was the whole Oxford Movement, with its many participants, that indelibly formed him into the person he was later on. As he said once, 'Rome did not make us Catholics, Oxford made us Catholics'. In the environs of Oxford, a unique and historical coming-together of gifted individuals led to enrichment, not only for Anglicanism, but also for the Catholic Church. Newman was the greatest fruit of that Movement, as well as being its principal inspiration – but he could only be so alongside others, who in their different ways helped him and supported him. Even with the sundering and rupture which followed, the friendships rekindled in later years speak of some greater unity beyond the Church estrangements, a more powerful overarching work of Gospel truth and love.

If these pages show anything, it is that grace was at work in the life of John Henry Newman. He was a person of humanity and faith. All his days, from the age of fifteen onward, he had travelled the road God set out before him, often in difficult and dark circumstances. His life is one of unfolding Catholic faith, already becoming paramount for him as an Anglican, and then reaching a fulfilment after 1845 in the actual Catholic Church itself. Despite its failings, and the arrogance it could display at an institutional level, and the cruelty, as he saw it, he yet believed in that Church. He saw it as the place where, in its prayer and worship, and through the lives of its people, there is carried in a special way the light of hope and healing for a needy world. As he once wrote about it, from his own experience, in a letter to Frederic Rogers:

> I have found in the Catholic Church abundance of courtesy, but very little sympathy, among persons in high place, except a few – but there is a depth and power in the Catholic religion, a fulness of satisfaction in its creed, its theology, its rites, its sacraments, its discipline, a freedom yet a support also, before which the neglect or the misapprehension about oneself on the part of individual persons, however exalted, is as so much dust, when weighed in the balance.[4]

That was in 1868. Subsequently, of course, there was the official honouring of him, when he was created a cardinal, and the cloud he still felt under lifted.

And now, in acknowledging him as among the blessed in heaven – surely that is no more than saying he is among all those he loved and accompanied in his lifetime – the Church is honouring him yet again. How appropriate it is that the ceremony of beatification should occur in England itself, at Crofton Park, near Birmingham, and close to Newman's beloved Rednal, where he had been laid to rest – and moreover to be conducted by the German theologian-Pope, Benedict XVI, who has freely acknowledged his own personal indebtedness to him. But he had already been recognised in a significant way back in 1963, during the third session of the Second Vatican Council, when

Pope Paul VI beatified the Passionist priest Dominic Barberi, who received him into the Church. At that ceremony in Rome, Paul VI singled him out for special mention, and, in words which still ring true, described Newman as

> him who, in full consciousness of his mission – 'I have a work to do' – and guided solely by love of the truth and fidelity to Christ, traced an itinerary, the most toilsome, but also the greatest, the most meaningful, the most conclusive, that human thought ever travelled during the last century, indeed one might say during the modern era, to arrive at the fulness of wisdom and peace.[5]

NOTES

1.   *The Month*, October 1890, pp. 154–6.
2.   *LD*, XXXII, pp. 601–2.
3.   Ibid., p. 588.
4.   *LD*, XXIV, pp. 24–5.
5.   Sermon on 27 Oct 1963, A.A.S. 55 (1963), p. 1025.

— APPENDIX —

Quotations from Selected Writings

From MEDITATIONS AND DEVOTIONS

CALLED BY NAME

1. God has created all things for good; all things for their greatest good; everything for its greatest good. What is the good of one is not the good of another; what makes one man happy would make another unhappy. God has determined, unless I interfere with His plan, that I should reach that which will be my greatest happiness. He looks on me individually, He calls me by my name, He knows what I can do, what I can best be, what is my greatest happiness, and He means to give it to me.

2. God knows what is my greatest happiness, but I do not ... Thus God leads us by strange ways; we know He wills our happiness, but we neither know what our happiness is, nor the way. We are blind; left to ourselves we should take the wrong way; we must leave it to Him.

3. Let us put ourselves into His hands, and not be startled though He leads us by a strange way, a *mirabilis via*, as the Church speaks. Let us be sure He will lead us right, that He will bring us to that which is, not indeed what we think best, nor what is best for another, but what is best for us.

Colloquy. O my God, I will put myself without reserve into Thy hands. Wealth or woe, joy or sorrow, friends or bereavement, honour or humiliation, good report or ill report, comfort or discomfort, Thy presence or the hiding of Thy countenance, all is good if it comes from Thee. Thou art wisdom and Thou art love – what can I desire more? Thou hast led me in Thy counsel, and with glory hast Thou received me. What have I in heaven, and apart from Thee what want I upon earth? My flesh and my heart faileth: but God is the God of my heart, and my portion for ever.

MY VOCATION IN LIFE

1. God was all-complete, all-blessed in Himself; but it was His will to create a world for His glory … We are all created to His glory – we are created to do His will. I am created to do something or to be something for which no one else was created; I have a place in God's counsels, in God's world, which no one else has; whether I be rich or poor, despised or esteemed by man, God knows me and calls me by my name.

2. God has created me to do Him some definite service; He has committed some work to me which He has not committed to another. I have my mission – I never may know it in this life, but I shall be told it in the next. Somehow I am necessary for His purposes, as necessary in my place as an Archangel in his – if, indeed, I fail, He can raise another, as He could make the stones children of Abraham. Yet I have a part in this great work: I am a link in a chain, a bond of connection between persons. He has not created me for naught. I shall do good, I shall do His work; I shall be an angel of peace, a preacher of truth in my own place, while not intending it, if I do but keep His commandments and serve Him in my calling.

3. Therefore I will trust Him. Whatever, wherever I am, I can never be thrown away. If I am in sickness, my sickness may serve Him; in perplexity, my perplexity may serve Him; if I am in sorrow, my sorrow

may serve Him. My sickness, or perplexity, or sorrow may be necessary causes of some great end, which is quite beyond us. He does nothing in vain; He may prolong my life, He may shorten it; He knows what He is about. He may take away my friends, He may throw me among strangers, He may make me feel desolate, make my spirits sink, hide the future from me – still He knows what He is about.

O Adonai, O Ruler of Israel, Thou that guidest Joseph like a flock, O Emmanuel, O Sapientia, I give myself to Thee. I trust Thee wholly. Thou art wiser than I – more loving to me than I myself. Deign to fulfil Thy high purposes in me whatever they be – work in and through me. I am born to serve Thee, to be Thine, to be Thy instrument. Let me be Thy blind instrument. I ask not to see – I ask not to know – I ask simply to be used.[1]

JESUS CHRIST THE SAME FOR EVER

1. All things change here below. I say it, O Lord; I believe it; and I shall feel it more and more the longer I live ... And, though I know not what Thou seest concerning me, so much I know, that Thou dost read in my life perpetual change. Not a year will leave me as it found me, either within or without. I never shall remain any time in one state. How many things are sure to happen to me, unexpected, sudden, hard to bear! I know them not. I know not how long I have to live. I am hurried on, whether I will it or no, through continual change. O my God, what can I trust in? ...

2. Everything short of Thee, O Lord, is changeable, but Thou endurest. Thou art ever one and the same ... Thou art the rarest, most precious, the sole good; and withal Thou art the most lasting. The creature changes, the Creator never. Then only the creature stops changing, when it rests on Thee. On Thee the Angels look and are at peace; that is why they have perfect bliss. They never can lose their blessedness, for they never can lose Thee. They have no anxiety, no

misgivings – because they love the Creator; not any being of time and sense, but 'Jesus Christ, the same yesterday and today, who is also for ever'.

3. My Lord, my Only god, '*Deus meus et omnia*', let me never go after vanities. '*Vanitas vanitatum et omnia vanitas.*' All is vanity and shadow here below. Let me not give my heart to anything here. Let nothing allure me from Thee; O keep me wholly and entirely. Keep Thou this most frail heart and this most weak head in Thy Divine keeping. Draw me to Thee morning, noon, and night for consolation. Be Thou my own bright Light, to which I look, for guidance and for peace. Let me love Thee, O my Lord Jesus, with a pure affection and a fervent affection! Let me love Thee with the fervour, only greater, with which men of this earth love beings of this earth. Let me have that tenderness and constancy in loving Thee, which is so much praised among men, when the object is of the earth. Let me find and feel Thee to be my only joy, my only refuge, my only strength, my only comfort, my only hope, my only fear, my only love.

AN ACT OF LOVE

1. My Lord, I believe, and know, and feel, that Thou art the Supreme Good. And, in saying so, I mean, not only supreme Goodness and Benevolence, but that Thou art the sovereign and transcendent Beautifulness. I believe that, beautiful as is Thy creation, it is mere dust and ashes, and of no account, compared with Thee, who art the infinitely more beautiful Creator … And I feel the truth of all this, in my own degree, because Thou hast mercifully taken our nature upon Thee, and hast come to me as man. '*Et vidimus gloriam ejus, gloriam quasi Unigeniti a Patre*' – 'and we saw His glory, the glory as it were of the only begotten of the Father'. The more, O my dear Lord, I meditate on Thy words, works, actions, and sufferings in the Gospel, the more wonderfully glorious and beautiful I see Thee to be.

2. And therefore, O my dear Lord, since I perceive Thee to be so beautiful, I love Thee, and desire Thee more and more. Since Thou art the One Goodness, Beautifulness, Gloriousness, in the whole world of being, and there is nothing like Thee, but Thou art infinitely more glorious and good than even the most beautiful of creatures, therefore I love Thee with a singular love, a one, only, sovereign love. Everything, O my Lord, shall be dull and dim to me, after looking at Thee. There is nothing on earth, not even what is most naturally dear to me, that I can love in comparison of Thee. And I would lose everything whatever rather than lose Thee. For Thou, O my Lord, art my supreme and only Lord and love.

3. My God, Thou knowest infinitely better than I, how little I love Thee. I should not love Thee at all, except for Thy grace. It is Thy grace which has opened the eyes of my mind, and enabled them to see Thy glory. It is Thy grace which has touched my heart, and brought upon it the influence of what is so wonderfully beautiful and fair. How can I help loving Thee, O my Lord, except by some dreadful perversion, which hinders me from looking at Thee? O my God, whatever is nearer to me than Thou, things of this earth, and things more naturally pleasing to me, will be sure to interrupt the sight of Thee, unless Thy grace interfere. Keep Thou my eyes, my ears, my heart, from any such miserable tyranny. Break my bonds – raise my heart. Keep my whole being fixed on Thee. Let me never lose sight of Thee; and, while I gaze on Thee, let my love of Thee grow more and more every day.[2]

From THE PAROCHIAL AND PLAIN SERMONS

WE BELONG TO GOD

We are not our own, any more than what we possess is our own. We did not make ourselves; we cannot be supreme over ourselves. We cannot be our own masters. We are God's property by creation, by redemption, by regeneration. He has a triple claim upon us. Is it not our happiness thus to view the matter? Is it any happiness, or any comfort, to consider we are *our* own? It may be thought so by the young and prosperous. These may think it a great thing to have everything, as they suppose, their own way – to depend on no one – to have to think of nothing out of sight – to be without the irksomeness of continual acknowledgement, continual prayer, continual reference of what they do to the will of another. But as time goes on, they, as all men, will find that independence was not made for man – that it is an unnatural state – may do for a while, but will not carry us on safely to the end. No, we are creatures; and, as being such, we have two duties, to be resigned and to be thankful.

Let us then view God's providences towards us more religiously than we have hitherto done. Let us try to gain a truer view of what we are, and where we are, in His kingdom. Let us humbly and reverently attempt to trace His guiding hand in the years which we have hitherto lived ... How did He cherish us as children! How did He guide us in that dangerous time when the mind began to think for itself, and the heart open to the world! ... How did He gently guide us towards the strait gate! How did He allure us along His everlasting way, in spite of its strictness, in spite of its loneliness, in spite of the dim twilight in which it lay! He has been all things to us.[3]

THE CALL OF CHRIST

... all through our life Christ is calling us. He called us first in Baptism; but afterwards also; whether we obey His voice or not, He graciously calls us still. If we fall from our Baptism, He calls us to repent; if we are striving to fulfil our calling, He calls us from grace to grace, and from holiness to holiness, while life is given us. Abraham was called from his home, Peter from his nets, Matthew from his office, Elisha from his farm, Nathaniel from his retreat; we are all in course of calling, on and on, from one thing to another ...

It were well if we understood this; but we are slow to master the great truth, that Christ is, as it were, walking among us, and by His hand, or eye, or voice, bidding us follow Him. We do not understand that His call is a thing which takes place now. We think it took place in the Apostle's days; but we do not believe in it, we do not look out for it in our own case. We have not eyes to see the Lord; far different from the beloved Apostle, who knew Christ even when the rest of the disciples knew Him not. When He stood on the shore after His resurrection, and bade them cast the net into the sea, 'that disciple whom Jesus loved saith unto Peter, It is the Lord' (Jn 21:7).[4]

PRAYING ALWAYS

To be religious is, in other words, to have the habit of prayer, or to pray always. This is what Scripture means by doing all things to God's glory; that is, so placing God's presence and will before us, and so consistently acting with a reference to Him, that all we do becomes one body and course of obedience, witnessing without ceasing to Him who made us, and whose servants we are; and in its separate parts promoting more or less His glory; according as each particular thing we happen to be doing admits more or less of a religious character. Thus religious obedience is, as it were, a spirit dwelling in us, extending its influence to every motion of the soul … they who have the true health and strength of soul, a clear, sober, and deep faith in Him in whom they have their being, will in all they do, nay (as St Paul says), even whether they 'eat or drink', be living in God's sight, or, in the words of the same Apostle in the text, live in ceaseless prayer … Our spiritual 'life' (as St Paul says) 'is *hid* with Christ in God' (Col 3:3) … Prayer is to spiritual life what the beating of the pulse and the drawing of the breath are to the life of the body. It would be as absurd to suppose that life could last when the body was cold and motionless and senseless, as to call a soul alive which does not pray. The state or habit of spiritual life exerts itself, consists, in the continual activity of prayer.[5]

THE GIFT OF THE SPIRIT,
A PORTION OF HEAVENLY GLORY

Such is the mysterious state in which Christians stand, if it be right to enlarge upon it. They are in Heaven, in the world of spirits, and are placed in the way of all manner of invisible influences. 'Their conversation is in heaven'; they live among Angels, and are within reach (as I may say) of the Saints departed. They are ministers round the throne of their reconciled Father, 'kings and priests unto God,' having their robes washed in the Lamb's blood, and being consecrated as temples of the Holy Ghost. And this being so, we have some insight into the meaning of St Paul's anxiety, that his brethren should understand 'the breadth and length', 'the riches' of the glorious inheritance which they enjoyed, and of his forcible declaration, on the other hand, that 'the natural man' could not 'discern' it.[6]

THE INDWELLING SPIRIT

The Holy Spirit causes, faith welcomes, the indwelling of Christ in the heart. Thus the Spirit does not take the place of Christ in the soul, but secures that place to Christ. St Paul insists much on this presence of Christ in those who have His Spirit ... The Holy Spirit, then, vouchsafes to come to us, that by His coming Christ may come to us, not carnally or visibly, but may enter into us. And thus He is both present and absent; absent in that He has left the earth, present in that He has not left the faithful soul; or, as He says Himself, 'The world seeth me no more, but *ye* see me'. (Jn 14:19)[7]

THE SPIRIT OF LOVE

We are Christ's, not by faith merely, nor by works merely, but by love ... We are saved, not by any of these things, but by the heavenly flame within us, which, while it consumes what is unseen, aspires to what is unseen. Love is the gentle, tranquil, satisfied acquiescence and adherence of the soul in the contemplation of God; not only a preference of God above all things, but a delight in Him because He is God, and because His commandments are good; ... it was Charity which brought Christ down. Charity is but another name for the Comforter. It is eternal Charity which is the bond of all things in heaven and earth; it is Charity wherein the Father and the Son are one in the unity of the Spirit; by which the Angels in heaven are one, by which all Saints are one with God, by which the Church is one upon earth.[8]

WATCHING FOR CHRIST

Now I consider this word *watching*, first used by our Lord, then by the favoured Disciple, then by the two great Apostles, Peter and Paul, is a remarkable word; remarkable because the idea is not so obvious as might appear at first sight, and next because they all inculcate it. We are not simply to believe, but to watch; not simply to love, but to watch; not simply to obey, but to watch; to watch for what? For that great event, Christ's coming ...

Do you know the feeling in matters of this life, of expecting a friend, expecting him to come, and he delays? ... Do you know what it is so to live upon a person who is present with you, that your eyes follow his, that you read his soul, that you see all its changes in his countenance, that you anticipate his wishes, that you smile in his smile, and are sad in his sadness, and are downcast when he is vexed, and rejoice in his successes? To watch for Christ is a feeling such as all these; as far as feelings of this world are fit to shadow out those of another.

He watches for Christ who has a sensitive, eager, apprehensive mind; who is awake, alive, quick-sighted, zealous in seeking and honouring Him; who looks out for Him in all that happens ...

And He watches *with* Christ, who, while he looks on to the future, looks back on the past, and does not so contemplate what his Saviour has purchased for him, as to forget what He has suffered for him. He watches with Christ, who ever commemorates and renews in his own person Christ's Cross and Agony, and gladly takes up that mantle of affliction which Christ wore here, and left behind Him when He ascended …

This then is to watch: to be detached from what is present, and to live in what is unseen; to live in the thought of Christ as He came once, and as He will come again; to desire His second coming, from our affectionate and grateful remembrance of his first. …

… You have to seek His face; obedience is the only way of seeking Him. All your duties are obediences. If you are to believe the truths He has revealed, to regulate yourselves by His precepts, to be faithful to His ordinances, to adhere to His Church and people, why is it, except because He has bid you? And to do what He bids is to obey Him, and to obey Him is to approach Him.[9]

OPENING OUR HEARTS

But there is another reason why God alone is the happiness of our souls, to which I wish rather to direct attention: – the contemplation of Him, and nothing but it, is able fully to open and relieve the mind, to unlock, occupy, and fix our affections. We may indeed love things created with great intenseness, but such affection, when disjoined from the love of the Creator, is like a stream running in a narrow channel, impetuous, vehement, turbid. The heart runs out, as it were, only at one door; it is not an expanding of the whole man. Created natures cannot open us, or elicit the ten thousand mental senses which belong to us, and through which we really live. None but the presence of our Maker can enter us; for to none besides can the whole heart in all its thoughts and feelings be unlocked and subjected. 'Behold', He says, 'I stand at the door and knock; if any man hear My voice and open the door, I will come in to him, and will sup with him and he with Me'. 'My Father will love him, and We will come to him, and make Our abode with him'. 'God hath sent forth the Spirit of His Son into your hearts'. 'God is greater than our heart, and knoweth all things'. (Rev 33:20. Jn 14:28. Gal 4:6. 1 Jn 3:20.) It is this feeling of simple and absolute confidence and communion, which soothes and satisfies those to whom it is vouchsafed. We know that even our nearest friends enter into us but partially, and hold intercourse with us only at times; whereas the consciousness of a perfect and enduring Presence, and it alone, keeps the heart open. Withdraw the Object on which it rests, and it will relapse again into its state of confinement and constraint; and in proportion as it is limited, either to certain seasons or to certain affections, the heart is straitened and distressed. If it be not over bold to say it, He who is infinite can alone be its measure; He alone can answer to the mysterious assemblage of feelings and thoughts which it has with it. 'There is no creature that is not manifest in His sight, but all things are naked and opened unto the eyes of Him with whom we have to do'. (Heb 4:13.)[10]

CHRIST 'EVER AT OUR DOORS'

Thus we are, at all times of the Gospel, brought close to His cross. We stand, as it were, under it, and receive its blessings fresh from it; only that since, historically speaking, time has gone on, and the Holy One is away, certain outward forms are necessary, by way of bringing us again under His shadow; and we enjoy these blessings through a mystery, or sacramentally, in order to enjoy them really.[11]

CHRIST, SOJOURNING HERE, PRESENT IN HEAVEN

And such in our measure shall we be, both in the appearance and in the reality, if we be His. 'Truly our fellowship is with the Father, and with His Son Jesus Christ' (1 Jn 1:3); but, as far as this world goes, shall we be of little account. 'The world knoweth us not, because it knew Him not' (1 Jn 3:1) ... Such is the condition of those who rise with Christ. He rose in the night, when no one saw Him; and we, too, rise we know not when nor how. Nor does any one know any thing of our religious history, of our turnings to God, of our growings in grace, of our successes, but God Himself, who secretly is the cause of them.[12]

That is our *home*; here we are but on pilgrimage, and Christ is calling us home. He calls us to His many mansions, which He has prepared. And the Spirit and the Bride call us too, and all things will be ready for us by the time of our coming. 'Seeing then that we have a great High Priest that has passed into the heavens, Jesus the Son of God, let us hold fast our profession' (Heb 4:14); seeing we have 'so great a cloud of witnesses, let us lay aside every weight' (Heb 12:1); 'let us labour to enter into our rest' (Heb 4:11); 'let us come boldly unto the Throne of Grace, that we may obtain mercy and find grace to help in time of need' (Heb 4:16).[13]

INTO PEACE AND PRAISE

All God's providences, all God's dealings with us, all His judgments, mercies, warnings, deliverances, tend to peace and repose as their ultimate issue ... after our soul's anxious travail; after the birth of the Spirit; after trial and temptation; after sorrow and pain; after daily dyings to the world; after daily risings unto holiness; at length comes that 'rest which remaineth unto the people of God'. After the fever of life; after wearinesses and sicknesses; fightings and despondings; languor and fretfulness; struggling and failing, struggling and succeeding; after all the changes and chances of this troubled unhealthy state, at length comes death, at length the White Throne of God, at length the Beatific Vision.[14]

BLESSEDNESS

Blessed are they who give the flower of their days, and their strength of soul and body to Him; blessed are they who in their youth turn to Him who gave His life for them, who would fain give it to them and implant it in them, that they may live for ever. Blessed are they who resolve – come good, come evil, come sunshine, come tempest, come honour, come dishonour – that He shall be their Lord and Master, their King and God! They will come to a perfect end, and to peace at the last.[15]

From THE DREAM OF GERONTIUS

Praise to the Holiest in the height,
And in the depth be praise,
In all His words most wonderful,
Most sure in all His ways.

O loving wisdom of our God!
When all was sin and shame,
A second Adam to the fight
And to the rescue came.

O wisest love! That flesh and blood
Which did in Adam fail,
Should strive afresh against the foe,
Should strive and should prevail;

And that a higher gift than grace
Should flesh and blood refine
God's Presence and His very self,
And Essence all-divine.

O generous love! That He who smote
In man for man the foe,
The double agony in man
For man should undergo;

And in the garden secretly,
And on the cross on high,
Should teach His brethren and inspire
To suffer and to die.[16]

NOTES

1. *Meditations and Devotions*, Longmans, Green and Co., 1953 edition, pp. 215–18.
2. Ibid., pp. 245–8.
3. *PS*, V, 'Remembrance of Past Mercies', pp. 83–4.
4. *PS*, VIII, 'Divine Calls', pp. 23–4.
5. *PS*, VII, 'Mental Prayer', pp. 206–7, 209.
6. *PS*, II, 'The Indwelling Spirit', pp. 229–30.
7. *PS*, VI, 'The Spiritual Presence of Christ in the Church', pp. 126–7.
8. *PS*, IV, 'Faith and Love', pp. 317–18.
9. Ibid., 'Watching', pp. 321–5, 332.
10. *PS*, V, 'The Thought of God the Stay of the Soul', pp. 317–19.
11. *PS*, VI, 'Waiting for Christ', p. 242.
12. Ibid., 'Rising with Christ', p. 216.
13. Ibid., 'Warfare the condition of Victory', p. 233.
14. Ibid., 'Peace in Believing', pp. 369–70.
15. *PS*, VIII, 'The Shepherd of our Souls', p. 243.
16. *Verses on Various Occasions*, pp. 363–4.

— BIBLIOGRAPHY —

Newman's Works
As mentioned at the beginning, the uniform edition of Newman's writings, which he arranged himself between 1869 and 1881, was published by Longmans, Green and Co. It went through many editions until the stock was destroyed in World War II. Some have been often republished subsequently, including the *Oxford University Sermons, Development of Doctrine, Apologia pro Vita Sua* and the *Grammar of Assent*, and with valuable introductory material. *The Idea of a University* has been published in various editions, the most recent by the UCD International Centre for Newman Studies, 2009, edited and with a preface by Teresa Iglesias. The posthumous *Meditations and Devotions* was often reissued, the best edition being that by Longmans, in 1953, with an introduction by Henry Tristram.

The website, 'Newman Reader – Works of John Henry Newman', is worth consulting: www.newmanreader.org

Some other publications of his works, relevant to this book, and with introductory material, include:

Coulson, John (ed.), *On Consulting the Faithful in Matters of Doctrine*, London: Geoffrey Chapman, 1961.
De Achaval, Hugo, and Holmes, J. Derek (eds), *The Theological Papers of John Henry Newman on Faith and Certainty*, Oxford: Clarendon Press, 1976.

Holmes, J. Derek, *The Theological Papers of John Henry Newman on Biblical Inspiration and on Infallibility*, Oxford: Clarendon Press, 1979.

Holmes, J. Derek, and Murray, Robert (eds), *On the Inspiration of Scripture*, London: Geoffrey Chapman, 1967.

Neville, William (ed.), *Addresses to Cardinal Newman with his Replies*, London: Longmans, Green and Co., 1905.

Tolhurst, James (ed.), *Sermon Notes of John Henry Newman 1849–1878*, Indiana: Notre Dame, 2000.

Tristram, Henry (ed.), *John Henry Newman: Autobiographical Writings*, New York: Sheed and Ward, 1956.

The *Letters and Diaries of John Henry Newman*, as has been stated, have now been completed in thirty-two volumes. They were started under the editorship of Charles Stephen Dessain, of the Oratory, in 1961. By the time of his death in 1976, volumes XI–XXXI were published, covering Newman's Catholic life. Since then, other editors have ensured that the Anglican period was covered, and with a final volume, XXXII, with added material, coming out in 2008. The Oxford University Press brought out the series from Volume XXIII onwards.

Biographies

Blehl, Vincent Ferrer, *Pilgrim Journey – John Henry Newman 1801–1845*, London: Burns and Oates, 2001.

Chisnall, Peter, *John Henry Cardinal Newman: A Man of Courage, Conflict and Conviction*, London: St Paul's, 2001. (A scholarly and concise recent offering.)

Dessain, C.S., *John Henry Newman*, London: Oxford University Press, 1980. (3rd edn). (Although a small book, it is by the Oratorian who was the greatest authority on Newman, and profoundly combines the strands of Newman's life and thought.)

Gilley, Sheridan, *Newman and his Age*, London: Darton Longman & Todd, 1990. (A standard, well-received book, and recently reprinted.)

Ker, Ian, *John Henry Newman*, Oxford: Oxford University Press, 1988. (Again, a highly acclaimed large biography, and recently reprinted.)

Martin, Brian, *John Henry Newman – His Life and Work*, London: Oxford University Press, 1982; also London and New York: Continuum, 2000.

Sugg, Joyce, *Ever Yours Affly – John Henry Newman and his Female Circle*, Leominster: Gracewing, 1996.

Trevor, Meriol, *Newman: The Pillar of the Cloud*, and *Newman: Light in Winter*, London: Macmillan, 1962. (This is the great and unsurpassed two-volume work on Newman's life and personality.)

— *Newman's Journey*, London: Fontana, 1974. (An abridged version of her two-volume biography of Newman's life.)

Ward, Wilfrid, *The Life of John Henry Cardinal Newman, Based on his Private Journals and Correspondence*, London: Longmans, Green and Co., 1912.

A worthwhile current Catholic Truth Society (London) booklet on his life is by Meriol Trevor and Leonie Caldecott, *John Henry Newman – Apostle to the Doubtful*, 2001.

Introductions to Newman's Life and Thought

Chadwick, Owen, *Newman – A Short Introduction*, London: Oxford University Press, 2010 (originally published in 1983).

Dulles, Avery, *John Henry Newman*, London: Continuum, 2002.

Ker, Ian and Merrigan, Terence, *The Cambridge Companion to John Henry Newman*, Cambridge: Cambridge University Press, 2009.

Lefebvre, Philippe and Mason, Colin (eds), *John Henry Newman – Doctor of the Church*, Oxford: Family Publications, 2007.

— *John Henry Newman in his Time*, Oxford: Family Publications, 2007.

Norris, Thomas, *Cardinal Newman for Today*, Dublin: Columba Press, 2010. (First published in 1996 as *Only Life Gives Life*.)

Strange, Roderick, *John Henry Newman: A Mind Alive*, London: Darton Longman and Todd, 2008.

The books by Thomas Norris and Roderick Strange are especially recommended, as is the masterly short work by Owen Chadwick, written from an Anglican perspective.

Some Specialised Contributions

Bastable, James (ed.), *Newman and Gladstone: Centennial Essays*, Dublin: Veritas Publications, 1978.

Coulson, John and Allchin, A.M., *The Rediscovery of Newman: An Oxford Symposium*, London: Sheed and Ward, SPCK, 1967.

Culler, Dwight A., *The Imperial Intellect: A Study of Newman's Educational Ideal*, New Haven: Yale University Press, 1955.

Fey, William R., *Faith and Doubt: The Unfolding of Newman's Thought on Certainty*, Sheperdstown, West Virginia: Patmos Press, 1976.

McGrath, Fergal, *Newman's University: Idea and Reality*, Dublin: Browne and Nolan, 1951.

McGrath, Francis, *John Henry Newman: Universal Revelation*, London: Burns and Oates, 1997; and Mulgrave, Victoria (Australia): John Garratt Publishing, 1997.

Murray, Placid Dom, *Newman the Oratorian*, Dublin: Gill and Macmillan, 1969; also Leominster: Fowler Books, 1980.

Strange, Roderick, *Newman and the Gospel of Christ*, London: Oxford University Press, 1981.

Vargish, Thomas, *Newman: The Contemplation of Mind*, Oxford: Clarendon Press, 1970.

Walgrave, J.H., *Newman the Theologian: The Nature of Belief and Doctrines Exemplified in His Life and Works*, trans. A.V Littledale, London: Geoffrey Chapman, 1960.

Fergal McGrath's book remains the definitive and most insightful study of Newman's years in Dublin, despite a lack of access to some sources which only became available later. A more recent and lively account is by Louis McRedmond, *Thrown Among Strangers*, Dublin: Veritas, 1990. There is extra material, including on Archbishop Cullen, in Collin Barr, *Paul Cullen, John Henry Newman, and the Catholic University of Ireland, 1845–1865*, Indiana: Notre Dame, 2003. (The characterisation of Newman here is shadowy, however, and suffers from the 'supersensitivity' stereotype.)

Extracts from Newman's Writings

Blehl, Vincent Ferrer (ed.), *Realisations – Newman's own Selection of his Sermons*, London: Darton Longman and Todd, 2009. (This is a welcome re-issue of a 1964 book, containing thirteen of Newman's best Anglican sermons.)

Sugg, Joyce (ed.), *A Packet of Letters – A Selection from the Correspondence of John Henry Newman*, Oxford: Clarendon Press, 1983.

Wilson, A.N. (ed.), *John Henry Newman: Prayers–Poems–Meditations*, London: SPCK, 2007. (This highly recommended work provides daily readings from Newman for a six-month period.)

There are two good current booklets from the Catholic Truth Society, London: *The Mind of Cardinal Newman* (compiled by C.S. Dessain), 1974, 2005; and *Daily Christian Living with John Henry Newman*, 2009.

Anglican and Oxford Themes

Battiscombe, Georgina, *John Keble – A Study in Limitations*, London: Constable, 1963.

Butler, Perry (ed.), *Pusey Rediscovered*, London: SPCK, 1983.

Chadwick, Owen, *The Spirit of the Oxford Movement – Tractarian Essays*, Cambridge: Cambridge University Press, 1990. (It includes valuable pages on Newman's Dublin University ideal: 'The University on Mount Zion', pp. 99-104.)

Church, R.W., *The Oxford Movement: Twelve Years 1833–1845*, London: Macmillan, 1891.

Dawson, Christopher, *The Spirit of the Oxford Movement*, London: Sheed and Ward, 1933.

Liddon, Henry Parry, *Life of Edward Bouverie Pusey*, 4 Vols, London: Longmans, Green and Co., 1897.

Middleton, R.D., *Newman and Bloxam: An Oxford Friendship*, London: Oxford University Press, 1947.

Much more could be listed on the indispensable field of Newman's Oxford and Anglican connections.

Some Related Historical Material

Ashton, Rosemary, *George Eliot – A Life*, London: Penguin, 1998.

Butler, Cuthbert Dom, *The Life and Times of Bishop Ullathorne 1806–1889*, 2 Vols, London: Burns, Oates and Washbourne, 1926.

Champ, Judith, *William Bernard Ullathorne – A Different Kind of Monk*, Leominster: Gracewing, 2006.

Fothergill, Brian, *Nicholas Wiseman*, London: Faber and Faber, 1963.

Hales, E.E.Y., *The Catholic Church in the Modern World*, London: Eyre and Spottiswoode, 1958.

— *Pio Nono – A Study in European Politics and Religion in the Ninteenth Century*, London: Eyre and Spottiswoode, 1954.

Potter, Matthew, *William Monsell of Tervoe 1812–1894*, Dublin: Irish Academic Press, 2009.

Reynolds, E.E., *Three Cardinals: Newman–Wiseman–Manning*, London: Burns and Oates, 1958.

— INDEX —

Month, The, 147, 149, 150, 163, 191

Morgan, Francis, 173

Moriarty, Bishop David, 95, 105, 164

Mozart, Wolfgang Amadeus, 184

Mozley, Anne, 176, 180, 184, 188

Mozley, Harriet (see Newman, Harriet)

Mozley, James Bowling, 49, 162, 184–5

Mozley, Jane (Janie), 153, 180

Mozley, Jemima (see Newman, Jemima)

Mozley, John, 36, 68, 153, 180

Mozley, Thomas, 36, 40, 52, 61, 65

Munich Brief, 128

Murphy, Mrs Mary (née Power), 182

Murray, Archbishop Daniel, 93, 95, 96, 104

Nardi, Mgr Francesco, 152

Napoleonic Wars, 16

Neville, William Paine, 130, 143, 176, 177, 185, 187, 188, 194

Newman, Charles, 15, 36, 133, 180

Newman, Elizabeth, 68, 98

Newman, Francis (Frank), 15, 21, 36, 133, 180

Newman, Harriet (Mrs Tom Mozley), 15, 32, 36, 40, 61, 97, 187

Newman, Jemima (née Fourdrinier), 15, 16, 26, 32, 36–7, 158–9, 176

Newman, Jemima (Mrs John Mozley), 15, 22, 32, 36, 48, 49, 53, 61, 68, 69, 77, 147, 153, 176, 180

Newman, John, 15, 16, 19, 20, 21, 36

Newman, John Henry,

Main events in his Anglican life: childhood, 15–6; evangelical conversion, 16–9; Trinity College, Oxford, 19; Oriel fellowship, 20–4; ordained deacon and priest, 20–1; appointed College Tutor, 21–2; Vicar of St Mary's, 23; Mediterranean tour,

27–9; initiating the *Tracts for the Times*, 31–2; his influence at its height, 32–4, 37–42; first doubts about his Anglican position, 45–7; *Tract 90* and consequences, 50–2, 54, 61; moving to Littlemore, 48–9, 53–4, 59–62; received into Catholic Church, 66–9.

Main events in his Catholic life: at Maryvale, 70, 75–6; stay in Rome, 76–80; ordination as Catholic priest, 80; beginning Oratorian vocation, 78–80; Oratory at Maryvale, 81–2; in Alcester Street, Birmingham, 84–6, 90; permanent Oratory on Hagley Road, 90–1, 102, 122–5; foundation of London Oratory, 86; Achilli case, 89–90, 94–8; Catholic University in Dublin, 93–7, 99–113, 116–20; estrangement between Birmingham and London Oratories, 113–16, 122; projected translation of the Bible, 123; editorship of the *Rambler* and consequences, 125–8; Oratory school, 123, 130–2, 150–2; the episode of the *Apologia*, 140–3; projected Oxford Oratory, 143–4, 150–2; preparing for, and writing the *Grammar of Assent*, 132–4, 159–63; Vatican Council I, 157, 163–8; honorary Fellow of Trinity, Oxford, 175–6, 179; made a Cardinal, 176–9; final controversies, 181–2; and death, 187–9.

Works published by him, cited in text: *Arians of the Fourth Century*, 26, 127; *Parochial and Plain Sermons*, 33–5 40–2, 48, 55–6, 158, 194; *Tracts for the Times* (contributions to), 31–2, 36, 45, 50–1; *Lyra Apostolica* (poems in), 37–8; *Prophetical Office of the Church*, 39; *Lectures on Justification*, 39–40; *Church of the Fathers*, 47–8; 'Letters of Catholicus', 49–50; *Tract 90*, 50–1, 54, 55, 61, 64–5, 128; *Oxford*